Speaking of Christianity

Books by Robert McAfee Brown
published by Westminster John Knox Press

The Bible Speaks to You

Liberation Theology: An Introductory Guide

Making Peace in the Global Village

Persuade Us to Rejoice: The Liberating Power of Fiction

Reclaiming the Bible: Words for the Nineties

Religion and Violence—Second Edition

Saying Yes and Saying No: On Rendering to God and Caesar

Spirituality and Liberation: Overcoming the Great Fallacy

Theology in a New Key: Responding to Liberation Themes

Unexpected News: Reading the Bible with Third World Eyes

Speaking
of Christianity

Practical Compassion, Social Justice, and Other Wonders

Robert McAfee Brown

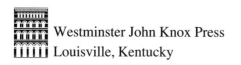 Westminster John Knox Press
Louisville, Kentucky

Book design by Jennifer K. Cox
Cover design by Kim Wohlenhaus
Cover illustration © Peter Hammer Verlag, Wuppertul/
Ass. para el desarrollo de Solentiname.

First edition
Published by Westminster John Knox Press
Louisville, Kentucky

This book is printed on acid-free paper that meets the
American National Standards Institute Z39.48 standard. ∞

PRINTED IN THE UNITED STATES OF AMERICA
97 98 99 00 01 02 03 04 05 06—10 9 8 7 6 5 4 3 2 1

Library of Congress Cataloging-in-Publication Data

Brown, Robert McAfee, date.
    Speaking of Christianity : practical compassion, social justice,
and other wonders / Robert McAfee Brown.—1st ed.
        p.   cm.
    Includes bibliographical references.
    ISBN 0-664-25742-9 (alk. paper)
    1. Christianity—20th century.   I. Title.
BR121.2.B734 1997
261.8—dc21   97-15534

It is not enough to experience the divine or the transcendent; the experience must then be incarnated in our behavior towards others. All the great religions insist that the test of true spirituality is practical compassion. The Buddha once said that after experiencing enlightenment [one] must leave the mountain top and return to the market place, and there practice compassion for all living beings. This also applies to the spirituality of a holy place. Crucial to the cult of Jerusalem from the very first was the importance of practical charity and social justice. The city cannot be holy unless it is also just and compassionate to the weak and vulnerable.

—Karen Armstrong, *Jerusalem*

Contents

Preface

I would give a great deal to have written the words of Karen Armstrong, reprinted on a preceding page. It would have demonstrated, to me at least, that I had a couple of realities firmly nailed down.

She is reminding us all that it is never enough to have a concept, let us say, or a commitment, nursed in solitude. It must always be *in relation to* something else. No matter how imperious the vision, there is always the obligation not to remain in an otherworldly resting place, but to reenter the human struggle as a caregiver, a purveyor of justice and mercy drawn from the largesse of one's newly acquired bounty.

For her, this is part of a universal religious demand, before which we are all held accountable. I agree, although my present purpose is less cosmic in scope than hers, and in the pages that follow it will be sufficient to explore this phenomenon within the demands of the Christian vision, reinforcing the universal claim that "the test of true spirituality is practical compassion." The insight is significant for us in the more prosaic attempt to give some content to the phrase "speaking of Christianity."

When we start a sentence with the phrase "speaking of Christianity," we have exposed ourselves to the possibility of wide areas of discourse. This may be a challenge so exacting that we dread it, but it is also a proposal whose attractiveness we cannot ignore. To be "speaking of Christianity" is to be open to employing the whole realm of speech with no fear of exhausting it. A quick glance at some of the topics treated below should provide ample evidence: puzzles, earthquakes, worship, martyrdom, beauty, sex, God, memory, politics, dissent, justice, compassion, ordinary men and extraordinary women, joy, bombers, anti-Semitism, ecology, evangelization, and cookbooks.

Such a list may in its own turn confront us with the charge of being dilettantes, skipping over immensely complicated matters, guilty of the charge

Preface

New Yorker Peter de Vries has immortalized: "On the surface he's brilliant, but way down deep he's shallow." But instead of becoming mired in theological guilt (probably Presbyterian in its origins), let us glory in the possibilities it opens up. For starters: we do not need to know everything. There are other folks around, and one person's lack may be another person's specialty. By the modest posture of listening, and not speaking too quickly, we may be guided into areas of knowledge previously denied us. It can even be the case (though this is not always pleasant) that a conversational partner may correct a lapse of ours, and call attention to it (this may be more pleasant) before the gaffe has been given a life of its own.

In other words, divining what we know and how we come to know it is an exacting and creative exercise. Enter it not with fear but with joy. It is not, except on rare occasions, to be indulged in solo, but in company with others. All are invited to join in the dance. Speaking of Christianity, that's a lot of its central message, right there.

Many of these chapters originated in talks or brief articles, and where that is important vis-à-vis the content, I have so indicated. About a third of them have not been printed before. I am grateful to the original publishers for permission to reprint in this format. In all cases, I have tried stylistically to retain the informality of the original presentations.

Part 1.
God, Sex, and Other Signs and Wonders

Does everybody read chapter 5 first? This is a non-issue. I am unconcerned about whether it is read first or last, so long as it is read in conjunction with what comes in between. In Part 1, let me admit, the order of the chapters is quite relaxed, and were I in a different mood or at a different time or place, they could have been arranged in a different order.

Let us make a virtue out of the "relaxed" order to introduce a type of order over the whole, namely, that the structure of Part 1 is also by design, a formal reminder that God can be encountered in all of the episodes that follow and in infinitely more episodes for which there is no space. God is present in the life of the mind, perhaps never more so than when confronting mystery; in the way we deal with catastrophe; in the unexpected possibilities of worship that departs the bounds of the expected; in the healing balm of music, even to college sophomores; in the challenge and creativity experienced in sexual relations that can empower and leave us rejoicing; and in the befores and afters of lives that are enshrouded in memory.

My hope is that together we can spread the net of appreciation and gratitude very wide, so that other simple, mundane experiences can also display the divine glory in the most humble receptacles, wonders not to be sneezed at but to be embraced with love.

1 Puzzles, Problems, and Mysteries

A problem is something which I meet, which I find complete before me, but which I am therefore to lay seige to and reduce. But a mystery is something in which I am myself involved. . . . A genuine problem is subject to an appropriate technique by the exercises of which it is defeated; whereas a mystery, by definition, transcends every conceivable technique. It is, no doubt, always possible . . . to degrade a mystery so as to turn it into a problem. But this is a fundamentally vicious proceeding.

—Gabriel Marcel,
in *Being and Having*

From time to time, as the mood strikes me, I become a crossword puzzle addict. Every day, during such moods, I confront a series of empty boxes and am challenged to fill them with appropriate letters, knowing that if I do so correctly the result will make sense. Not many things in life fit together as coherently or tidily as a crossword puzzle. Where else do words communicate both vertically and horizontally at the same time? Now and then (about once a day), I need some reminder that I do not live in a universe of total caprice, and crossword puzzles do the job.

I must live by the rules and conventions of the game if I expect to solve the puzzle. An abbreviation in the clue signals that an abbreviated form of the word goes in the box. A question mark after the clue hints at a play on words in the answer. Doing the vertical clues first helps the incompleted horizontal words to jump out more easily than if I reverse the procedure. A clue like "tributary in Upper Volta" indicates that the creator of the puzzle was getting desperate, and I feel morally justified in consulting

Originally published in *Christianity and Crisis*, August 1988. Used by permission.

an atlas. "German industrial city" is almost always going to be "Essen," because vowels and *s*'s are a puzzle constructor's greatest helpers. A passing acquaintance with foreign languages is also a help; for example, "uno follower" will always be "dos," and "to be, Fr.," will always be "être."

Crossword puzzles, then, exemplify a universe with consistent rules. The rules work. If you ignore them or try to cheat on them, they will finally trip you up and leave your puzzle in disarray. But if you abide by them and trust them (and are diligent enough), you can usually solve the puzzle. If you can't completely solve it, at least you will know that it *is* solvable — see tomorrow's paper. Once you read the answers to clues that remained elusive, you say, "Oh, of course!" How could you not have thought of that? The universe is still coherent. Better the fault be in us than in the stars, dear Brutus.

One other thing about crossword puzzle addiction: As long as you have not finished the puzzle, it is utterly absorbing. Calls to meals are ignored or responded to only grudgingly. Never are marriages under such severe threat as in those moments when it looks as though the final corner of the puzzle is doable and dinner will simply have to wait.

But once the puzzle has been solved, its charm disappears in a trice. Unless casually left on the coffee table so that someone can take notice and commend you for your skill and perseverance, the puzzle is put aside. No longer a challenge or threat, the completed puzzle becomes a cipher in your life and almost immediately is forgotten. But you emerge with a little higher self-esteem.

Do theologians, I sometimes wonder, gravitate to crossword puzzles (and detective stories) for the very reason that these human artifacts do not leave a residue of mystery or a cloud of unknowing, but exemplify worlds with no leftover loose ends? How often is such a penchant for tidiness and order fulfilled in the theological realm? My answer to that question: never. And the reason, I believe, is one that can be consoling not only to professional theologians but to all who wrestle with theological issues, which means everybody.

In wanting to spread out the precision of a crossword puzzle across the universe at large, we are confusing puzzles (or "problems" as Gabriel Marcel, a French existentialist, calls them) with mysteries. Our very vocabulary betrays us here. We talk, for example, about the "problem" of evil, as though evil could be dealt with in the same way we deal with a crossword puzzle. If evil is simply a "problem," we can search for a "solution," and when we have found a solution we can set the problem aside, confident that it will plague us no more.

But evil, we soon discover, never consents to being reduced to the status of a problem. A *mystery,* it defies coherent resolution—not just in the sense of being unknowable, but in the sense of being part of the unfathomable depth in our lives that we will never fully understand, but with which we will have to deal as long as we live. It will continue to haunt us, to threaten us, to defy us, and the closest we will ever get to understanding it are "hints and guesses" (as T. S. Eliot has called them). Rather than dispelling the mystery, they will *draw us into it,* so that we have to confront not only that mystery but other mysteries as well.

The most significant confrontation, perhaps, will be with the mystery of love, which likewise can never be fully understood. Often, perhaps most of the time, the mystery of love becomes terribly threatened by the mystery of evil. Sometimes, however, love does battle with evil and there will be pain but not necessarily total defeat. Sometimes love can draw good even out of the evil.

To make such affirmations is not to be suggesting solutions to a problem, but proposing that there can be enrichments to our partial understanding of a mystery. And those enrichments can sometimes be a blessing to just the degree that we do not succumb to what Marcel calls the "vicious proceeding" of trying to reduce them to the level of solutions.

Let the addiction to puzzles stand, therefore, so long as we do not mistakenly confuse it with a model of the real universe we inhabit.

2 Earthquakes and Aftershocks
Living Unwillingly on the Edge of Catastrophe

It has been three days now since the earthquake. The seismologists tell us it wasn't the "Big One" we've been expecting since 1906. The Big One is still to come. But there is not a soul out here who wouldn't settle for 6.9 on the Richter scale as an adequate expression of "bigness."

This is not a report of personal heroics on my part, or close brushes with death by others. Such accounts will have come from someone else. This is simply an initial series of reactions by one who happened to be located on the edge of catastrophe, not fully involved but definitely not detached either. Earthquakes come abruptly, so let us begin abruptly:

1. *Everyone has a story.* Every person within fifty miles of the encounter can tell you exactly what he or she was doing on September 17, 1989, at 5:04 P.M., just half an hour before the third game of the World Series was scheduled to start.

That is one of the things a "6.9 on the Richter scale" does: it delivers a universal event that everyone experiences from a personal perspective. The stories have to be told: "I was on the Bay Bridge when my car started to sway and I thought I had two flat tires. If I hadn't stopped right away I'd have gone over the section that had just broken off." Or, "I was cashing a check at the bank and all of a sudden the chandeliers started to dance, and I thought one of them was going to fall on me." Or, "I was in the operating room when the power went off and the floor heaved. Thank God we had a generator of our own, or the patient would

Originally published in *Christianity and Crisis,* November 1989. Used by permission.

have died." Or even, "If I'd gone onto the Cypress Structure on I-880 two minutes earlier, I'd have been crushed to death."

There is a democratizing tendency and a wiping out of class distinctions in all this. Earthquakes, like Yahweh, are no respecters of persons. The lowliest can have as chilling or thrilling a story as the most privileged. Life is a fabric of narrations bound between hard covers. The earthquake will remain a particularly vivid, perhaps the most vivid, chapter in the whole book.

2. *Life is capricious.* That seems to be the common thread in most of the stories, whether stated or not. Sooner or later there is a moment when it is asserted, "If I hadn't had to make that telephone call first . . ." or "If I hadn't turned off the freeway when I did, because I'd forgotten my briefcase . . ." or "If I hadn't been in the garden when the living room ceiling collapsed . . ." The conclusion to all of these conditional clauses is definitive: "*I'd be dead.*"

In our soberest moments we already know that life is capricious: this one got AIDS, that one didn't; this one had a six-year remission from cancer, that one was dead in two months; this one got a seat on the plane that crashed because of a no-show just before departure time; that one arrived too late to get on. We can put the capriciousness on hold much of the time, but after an earthquake it won't go away, and we can even extract a blessing from it which goes like this: savor the moments you have before they disappear, maybe forever; appreciate relationships to the full right now before they are lost; get that letter of appreciation off in the mail today; don't let the sun go down on your anger.

An acknowledgment of the capriciousness of life can also help us avoid trying to draw the divine design too neatly and coherently. At best, we have a God who sustains us through disasters not of God's choosing; at worst, we have a capricious God, who is worthy only of scorn and never of reverence.

3. *Crises bring out the best and the worst in us.* This is a cliché if there ever was one, but how nobly—and ignobly—its truth shines forth when things actually go to pieces. Within minutes after the Cypress Structure of I-880 caved in, people in Oakland were bringing ladders from backyards to climb up and see if they could drag survivors from the rubble—this at a

time when every fallen section could easily have engaged in further convulsions and rendered the rescuers as dead as those they were hoping to rescue. A bus driver stopped just short of the yawning gap on the floor of the Bay Bridge, herded his passengers back from the metal and concrete fissure, and then approached it alone, saving the lives of two men whose car was sickeningly poised on the very edge, between the roadway and the bay below.

And, just to keep the ledger balanced, the next morning there were reports of over one hundred arrests in San Francisco for looting.

The place where the cliché evaporates is the realization that we can never be sure ahead of time whether a catastrophe would bring out the best or the worst in *us*. My biggest problem was to keep my balance in the middle of an undulating parking lot, once I had figured out why my VW bug was dancing up and down as though a giant fist were pummelling it. But how would I have done if I'd been at the desk where I am writing now, and all the books that cascaded down on an empty desk had cascaded down on me? Would I have screamed or panicked or frozen, instead of obeying the basic rule in such situations: get under the damn desk? A friend did have the books cascade, and did get under the desk, and she simultaneously coaxed a frightened colleague to join her. Would that have occurred to me?

4. *It's more terrifying afterward.* On the whole, people rise to heights of coping at the moment of disaster in ways that frequently astonish them afterward. The adrenaline goes into overdrive and the numbness, paradoxically, helps too. But after the adrenaline and the numbness come the shakes: "What if I had started down the stairs (that collapsed)?" "What if I'd been buried in rubble and they never came to get me out?" Even more conducive to the shakes are the wider questions: "What was it like for the people trapped with mangled bodies, knowing they would die painfully?" "What if my wife (or husband or friend or brother or sister or cousin or aunt or uncle) had been inside a falling building?" The fears are greater a week later than a few hours later, as the many possible consequences and courses of action, some fulfilled and some averted, are weighed and assessed in all those nights when we cannot sleep. There is a diabolical conspiracy between these human "aftershocks" and the geological aftershocks that con-

tinue for days, sometimes approaching the original quake in intensity. Each validates the worst fears prompted by the other.

Here is where the therapy sessions, and the group discussions, and the reenacting of what was experienced, become so important. Two of our grandchildren, home at the time of the quake, were able the next day (most schools being closed) to "play" earthquake with piles of pillows, diving in and out of them, and resolving some of their immediate fears of being buried in rubble. One of them, a seven-year-old, had a ball walking around "heaven" and repeating "Hi, God. Hi, Jesus. Hi, Mary."

5. *Priorities are clarified.* The loss of the shiny new car is nothing, so long as the family is safe. The loss of a house may be a financial and even psychic disaster, but it can be borne when there has been no loss of those who share life within the house. Survival of business inventories are secondary to the survival of the workforce that checks the inventories. Remember, the massive overload on the phone lines after the quake had subsided was not caused by people trying to check how the stockmarket was responding. Those on the scene were calling those off the scene to reassure them that they were all right, while those off the scene were calling those on the scene to be reassured that they were all right.

From this, we gain a sense of what is important and what is not important. Baseball, for example, is not important, while friends and family remain important. This was as true for the ballplayers poised for game three of the World Series, as for the forty-two thousand fans in Candlestick Park waiting to watch them. When the quake began, the players looked for their wives and children in the stands above them, not for mitts and bats, the tools of their trade. Almost everybody in the baseball world, from the commissioner down to the coaches, realized that the status of the World Series was a trivial item on the human agenda. The Oakland A's even announced that if the series were continued, and if the A's won, there would be no champagne party afterward, at least not on television. Many fans and a lot of players felt it would be a sacrilege to continue the Series, just as continuing the Olympic Games in Munich after the Israeli athletes were murdered had been a sacrilege.

6. *Life goes on.* This was the favorite argument for *continuing* the World Series. While newspaper headlines were exaggerating the claim after two

days that "Life in San Francisco is Returning to Normal," it is true that a state of absolute crisis soon subsides. Rubble is removed, condemned buildings are demolished, schools reopen, electrical power returns to the financial district, computers are up rather than down. People cope. The resilience of the human spirit in the face of such catastrophe is awesome and has always been so. In the Warsaw ghetto—to make a quantum analogical leap—where for years and not just for moments life was in jeopardy, the report is clear: schools were started; bar mitzvahs were held; young people fell in love, married, and had children; barter systems were established; Torah was studied; God was worshiped; guns were smuggled. Time does not "heal all wounds," but time demands that we move on, make new beginnings, cherish whatever happy memories there are, and confront bitter memories with more than bitterness. Extraordinary.

7. *We're in it together.* The most amazing bonding takes place. Strangers gather on the sidewalks when the shock waves cease. They talk to one another. Many times they hug. Nominal neighbors are suddenly real neighbors coping together with a broken water main. In downtown areas people appear with food. Trained individuals are suddenly on the scene with information about shelters, blankets, first aid. Stories are exchanged ("Where were you?" "Where were *you*?"), suggestions are offered ("You won't be able to get to work that way because they just announced over the radio that part of I-80 is closed north of Emeryville. Now if you switch over to San Pablo Avenue . . ."). A group of friends gathers in mutual support outside by candlelight (better not light candles inside because the gas might be leaking). In whatever situation, the chemistry is at work. Better yet, the alchemy is at work, that magic transformative power that turns leaden human beings into pure gold.

8. *Nobody's blaming God . . . yet.* After three days of round-the-clock television, I had yet to hear anyone holding God directly responsible. They began to do so, of course, as the numbness wore off, and particularly as the anger increased. Somebody's got to be held responsible and take the blame. "What kind of a God would let this happen?"

Without trying to develop a theodicy in twenty-five words or more, I am constrained to say that it will be a gain to be rid of any lingering notion of an omnipotent God who wills everything that happens. A God who would directly will the collapse of an interstate highway on randomly selected individuals at the height of the rush hour would be a moral monster. If there is any place in all the mess where we can assume that God is present, it is surely among the victims, entering into their suffering with them, helping them to bear it, and sustaining them with immense reservoirs of love.

There is no period in human history when the anguished cry has not gone up, "Why . . . why . . . why?" Confronting the earthquake with this question does not mean that dealing with the relationship of God to evil is being raised for the first time, but that a universal mystery for the human spirit is now being faced in very local terms, which are the only terms on which it can authentically be raised.

Indeed, during the immediate recovery from the disaster, the question "Why?" may be premature, and even a luxury in which we should not yet indulge. What, then, should people of faith be doing? The answer is not hard to find. They should not be speculating just yet. They should be binding up the wounds of the injured, feeding the hungry, opening churches and synagogues to the homeless, helping those who have freaked out learn how to cope with tonight and tomorrow and next week. Those with technical expertise should be drawing plans for a new two-level freeway that won't collapse, or insisting to the authorities that two-level freeways are now obsolete. Those with reportorial gifts should be collecting stories of the triumph of the human spirit, to remind us not only now but when the next catastrophe occurs that even in the face of the implacable and impersonal forces of nature, there is a part of that nature, called "human nature," that is not implacable but malleable, not impersonal but personal, the part that everlastingly refuses to be daunted or to give up, especially when disaster strikes.

3 Worship

Piece of Cake or Subversion?

I initially thought that reflecting on the theme of "freedom for worship" would be easy. Indeed, it seemed pretty tame: freedom for worship is the cornerstone of democracy and our nation's greatness.

Nobody in *our* land is going to object to people getting together to pray and sing and read the Bible unless they are exceptionally raucous, and "raucous" is not an adjective frequently associated with Presbyterians like myself. *We* do things "decently and in order." We Americans, because we worship God at the drop of a hat, must be God-lovers, and therefore entitled to special privileges both now and forever more. Amen. Piece of cake.

I want, however, to turn the topic around, and suggest that freedom for worship isn't all that tidy. It can get us into a peck of trouble if we take it seriously.

This became clear to me during a trip to the Philippines in 1989, when I suggested in a lecture that it was the task of the church to be subversive, not in the cloak-and-dagger sense, but in the true meaning of the word, which comes from the Latin *vertere,* to overthrow, to overturn, to start things in a new direction. There can be a *super*-version, which means to overturn from above (as in the belief that if you can convert the captains of industry to Jesus Christ, capitalism will become moral), and there can be *sub*-version, overturning from below (which means working at the grass roots, relying on what liberation theologian Gustavo Gutiérrez calls "the power of the poor in history" or writing a novel called *Uncle Tom's Cabin).*

Originally presented at a church conference in Tampa, Florida, in 1989; published in *Church and Society* (PHEWA), 1989.

worship

In a world of few certainties, one certainty we can count on is that radical changes in our society are not going to be initiated from above. Those with power are not interested in sharing it; they are interested in only consolidating it. They will do whatever is necessary to keep things as they are. Change will have to come from below, from those who initially appear powerless, but who can risk a lot because they have so little to lose.

So, at least, I tried to suggest in Manila. What I did not learn, unfortunately, until after the talk was that the Filipino government had taken to labeling churches and individual church leaders as "subversives," and therefore candidates for the roving death squads, whenever these subversives oppose government policies, or support land reform, or demand the release of political prisoners.

I could not help wondering how long it has been since anyone accused an American church of being subversive. Bland, yes; irrelevant, much of the time; elitist, frequently; lumbering, mostly; supporter of the status quo, right on target. But subversive? No way.

Suppose we wanted to engender a little subversion in our national life and in our church life. How could we go about it? By urging "freedom for worship." Let us develop this unlikely proposal.

1. *Freedom for worship is subversive because it opens the door to doubt and keeps us off balance.* If you are off balance, you find yourself going in totally unexpected directions. Look at Psalms 42 and 43. Here is the declaration of a worshiper par excellence, right in the midst of the worshipbook of the Hebrew scriptures. It's about thirsting for God, leading liturgical processions, offering glad shouts and songs of thanksgiving to the deity, celebrating festivals, bowing to the altar, playing the lyre—worship at its most reassuring. People who can do all that must really have it together.

But within this glorious outburst are dark moments, despairing phrases about tears, about the taunts of those who mock, "Where *is* your God anyway?" about mourning, about being cast down and disquieted, about having been forgotten by God, about hoping that someday things will be better, because today is sure the pits.

These two moods are interspersed throughout the psalms—high moments alternating with low moments, the low moments winning out so the

13

final words are no more than a cry of hope that maybe, just maybe, in the future it will be better.

Conclusion? Worship does not bring tidy assurances. If it sometimes takes us close to the divine presence, it also gives us a vision that is not very frequently sustained in the ongoing moments of life. If God is sometimes close, then when God is far away, God is *much* farther away, precisely because of the previous closeness. Here, as elsewhere, the higher we rise, the farther we fall. We might formulate a statement to go on the cover of every order of worship:

> Warning: the Surgeon General
>   has determined that worship
>   may be hazardous to your faith.

Let us call on another Jewish source, the Hasidic tradition, to seal the point:

It is during the occupation of Middle Europe. A town is captured by the Nazis. The beadle (janitor) goes into the empty synagogue the next morning, climbs the bimah (pulpit), and says, fervently, "Lord God, Creator of the universe, I have come to tell you that we are still here."

The Nazis seal off a ghetto and then deprive the victims of food and water. Once again the beadle mounts the bimah and prays, "Lord God, Creator of the universe, I have come to tell you that we are still here."

The Nazis rape the Jewish women and send the Jewish men, women, and children in cattle cars to Auschwitz. Only the beadle is left. He climbs the bimah of the empty synagogue and prays, "Lord God, Creator of the universe, I have come to tell you that I am still here. . . . But you, Lord God, creator of the universe, *where are you?*"

2. *Freedom for worship is subversive because it demands inclusiveness, and that makes us uneasy.* Look at Isaiah 56:3–8, which unmasks insensitivity, or at best naïveté, on the part of those for whom "freedom for worship" is still a piece of cake. A recent church conference listed working

titles on the theme of "freedom for worship": AIDS prevention, criminal justice, inclusive language, the disabled, racial and ethnic inclusiveness, drug addiction, mental illness, refugees, and lesbian and gay support.

What do all those topics have in common? They all involve people who cannot take "freedom for worship" for granted. If they have it, they had to fight to get it, and they have to fight to keep it. If they don't have it, they are still fighting to get it. Whether they have it or don't have it, the possession is fragile. People with AIDS, people with criminal records, drug addicts, people with mental and physical impairments, refugees, lesbians, gays—these are not exactly at the top of the list of those the rest of us go out to recruit in membership drives, and they are hardly on the list at all as nominees for elder and deacon positions.

As a further reminder that we cannot build denominational or creedal or racial fences around ourselves when we worship, there is a disturbing point in Isaiah 56, in which God says in no uncertain terms that an admission ticket for worship is given to everyone—repeat, everyone—who keeps the Sabbath and honors the covenant. In case there is any doubt left in the minds of the devout, God goes on to say, with exquisite explicitness, that this includes "foreigners" who might be Egyptians, Assyrians, or Babylonians (to name the "evil empires" of the ancient world); the eunuchs (who were not high on the social register of the Jerusalem Four Hundred); the outcasts (undesirable riffraff); and in the most threatening phrase of all, "yet others besides those already gathered"—all the unindicted co-conspirators, and any old persons lounging around the city streets, exercising their right to freedom of assembly by opting to sleep on the outdoor grates of the city's heating system.

This is doing things "decently and in order"? According to Isaiah, the doors are open, the gates are unbarred. Anybody is welcome. Talk about subversion. And to summon yet another Hasidic tale, this open-arms policy of celestial nondiscrimination is engineered from the divine throne itself.

It is a day of rejoicing in heaven. There has been a great victory. The children of Israel have escaped across the Red Sea, whose waters have risen to engulf the pursuing Egyptians and drown them all. Not only a great victory, but a Jewish victory to boot, and how many Jewish victories has heaven ever had a chance to celebrate? So there is much rejoicing in heaven. The angels are dancing. A feast is being prepared.

And then Raphael, one of the archangels, looks at the divine throne. God is not only not rejoicing; God is weeping.

The archangel is mystified. So he goes over, kneels before the divine throne, and says, "Lord God, Creator of the universe, it is a time of celebration, a time of singing and dancing. Why are you weeping?"

And from the divine throne comes the anguished voice of the Lord God, Creator of the universe: "Why should I not be weeping, when so many of *my children* have drowned?"

3. *Freedom for worship is subversive because it acknowledges God's worth-ship, and there is no end to that.* This is a favorite sermonic wordplay: worship equals worth-ship. It is usually employed to highlight what we like to call the "vertical" dimension of worship, addressed to God, rather than the "horizontal" dimension of worship, which begins to sound suspiciously like all that social-action stuff.

But quite the contrary, the notion of God's "worth-ship," rather than being a narrowing or exclusive concern, turns out to be a broadening and inclusive concern, in which "all that social-action stuff" is alarmingly center stage.

A full acknowledgment of God's worth-ship involves a recognition of the worth of all God's creation, God's creatures, everything that God has created; the world in which people engage in acts of devotion but are also devastated by personal infidelities and acts of corporate injustice; a world of great human possibilities and terrible waste of human life; a world ripe for concerns about health, education, and welfare, and yet rife with their opposites—disease, illiteracy, and exploitation. Concern about God's worth-ship carries with it the territory of concern about the worth-ship of God's handiwork, affirming and supporting all that is good, opposing and combating all that has gone sour. If people say they love God and hate their brothers and sisters, the First Letter of John says flat out, they are liars.

But there is another and even more important reason why acknowledging God's worth-ship is subversive. The acknowledgment of God's true "worth" sets God in a category belonging to no one else, and makes it impossible to acknowledge the unique worth of any other god who vies for our allegiance. We cannot examine all the other deities in our humanly created pantheon, so let us concentrate on the god who most powerfully beckons us today and wants our all-out support. I have no doubt who that God is. It is the god of the nation-state, of our whole political/economic structure, the god who most aggressively demands our unqualified allegiance, who says, in words stolen from another context, "You shall have no other gods before me." And in this particular period of our own history, the god who asks such uncritical allegiance is not only making a pitch for a certain kind of political order but for a certain kind of economic order as well.

Preachers, check it in your parishes. You could voice doubts about many formulations of the doctrine of the Trinity, or the eternality of hell, or the inspiration of scripture, or the mechanism for the transmission of original sin, and scarcely cause a ripple of concern. But raise a question about the morality of market capitalism, or the right of the United States to dictate the economic policies of Central American states, or our track record of support for dictatorships throughout the world during the latter half of the twentieth century, and your job may well be on the line.

As an abstract proposition, it sounds so simple: to worship the God of justice is to opt for justice in the political and economic sphere. Given specificity it means such things as supporting the total funding of government programs for Women, Infants, and Children, opposing an increase in the Pentagon budget, challenging those who say that "America is the envy of the world," refusing to accede to the notion that to affirm oneself as a "liberal" makes one unpatriotic, supporting moves for the forgiveness of the third-world debt, and so on. We can quibble over the details, and our lists won't always coincide, but there will be agreement on what motivates the lists, namely, that when we are denied the right to criticize our nation's political and economic policies, we had better refuse to accept such restrictions, lest we thereby enlist in the service of a rival deity, the nation, that rival deity who is really a false god, an idol.

And idolatry, rather than being a quaint biblical notion about *ba'als* or totem poles or sacred stones, is probably the most up-to-date notion in the entire Bible. (If you need still further convincing about such matters, try Richard Shaull's *Naming the Idols: Biblical Alternatives for U.S. Foreign Policy* [Meyer-Stone Books, Oak Park, Illinois, 1988].)

We saw idolatry in the acclaim given to Adolf Hitler, and more recently to Ferdinand Marcos—and we had better see it in ourselves as well, branding other nations, not our own nation, as "evil empires," or putting emphasis on the mechanical exercise of *reciting* the Pledge of Allegiance rather than on *implementing* its radical claim of "liberty and justice for *all*" instead of just for some. A recent presidential candidate said, "I will never criticize the United States of America," but this is an absolutely impossible attitude for the rest of us, unless we too wish to bow the knee to the nation-state instead of to the God who is above every nation-state, and before whom every nation-state is weighed and found wanting.

4. *Freedom for worship is subversive because it involves demands as well as assurances.* Who has not heard a sermon about worship as something "to comfort the afflicted and afflict the comfortable"? Both are necessary, but here I will concentrate on the fact that worship not only contains assurances but inflicts demands. What a shock to go from the assurance that God loves us to the *demand* that therefore we must love our neighbors (those quite unlovable folk down the block) and even love our enemies (those absolutely impossible people who are threatening the American way of life).

I know of no one who faced this more directly than Moses, who had that fantastic "worship experience" (as we like to say) in the desert and found that as a result he had to move in the very uncomfortable direction of going back to Egypt and taking on the royal establishment. He discovered that there was a direct connection between seeing a burning bush in the desert and becoming a political firebrand back home . . .

And here I propose to play a mean trick on the reader. Sooner or later, all of us have to accept the fact that the demands are directed *to us,* and not just to some third party to transmit to us. So finally we're really on our own.

Nothing to help us but the Bible. No more ultimate resource than the folks surrounding us, and the realization that the demands finally lead right to our own doorstep and haven't been missent.

So the query is now addressed to you: *Why* is freedom to worship so subversive?

The ball is in your court. Give it your best shot.

4 Encounter with Beauty
A Musical Reminiscence

Flying home after a frustrating week of air travel, I finally put aside a briefcase full of unfinished work and tuned into American Airlines's musical entertainment, Mozart's Symphony Number 40 in G Minor (K. 550), the "ever-popular Fortieth Symphony," I believe the announcer called it.

"Ever popular," indeed. Instead of lifting me out of myself into timeless delight, as Mozart is supposed to do, it plunged me back immediately into the time of delight when I had first discovered it as an Amherst freshman, many years earlier, in Music 1, a course in which Vincent Morgan dissected Mozart sufficiently for me to begin a lifelong friendship with his music.

I could carry a tune sufficiently well to make the Amherst choir, and had once been in the fourth row of the second violin section of the Binghamton Central High School Orchestra. I remember banging out the rudimentary symphonic themes on various pianos that year at Amherst before Music 1 tests, as we strove to distinguish between exposition, development, and recapitulation in Mozart's Fortieth, Beethoven's Fifth, Sibelius's Fifth, and other brand-new fare that Music 1 served up to eager auditors.

Those without quick ears for a telltale nuance or a predictable oboe entrance would sometimes devise rhymes to identify the musical themes. We were told by Professor Vincent Morgan that such student shortcuts should be rejected, since they could easily kill the music forever, the melody inextricably linked to the doggerel. To little avail. A moderately tone-deaf but linguistically

Originally published in the Amherst College Fiftieth Class Anniversary book, May 1993.

gifted junior, for example, had supplied a way to make it through the latter part of Mozart. The trio of the third movement could be sung flawlessly to the words, "This is the *tr*-io, this is the *tr*-io, of *Moz*art's *sym*-phon-*y*." And when we got to the first theme of the finale, the spot on the midterm could always be identified if sung to the words, "O, *Moz*-art's almost *o*-ver, let him *quit,* let him *quit,* let him *quit,*" provided you repeated the phrase and gave "quit" an almost imperceptible two-syllable inflection.

The point of recounting this nonsense is to insist that we all got beyond it, and to suggest that during the four years we were at Amherst, Music 1 pretty well transformed the musical tastes of a college generation.

I had been led to believe in my high school days that college dormitory life would be one unending cacophony of noisy phonographs. But the longer I was around, the more I began to hear the *B Minor Mass,* or the *"Jupiter" Symphony* coming out of fraternity windows or South College stairwells.

And it was increasingly true that as a generation of musical literates began to emerge, more than just the "required listening" for Music 1 could be heard. He who was stirred by the vigor of Brahms's First naturally and painlessly moved to the pastoral Brahms Second. To untangle Beethoven's Fifth, a relatively easy job—earned one the right to go on to his Third, a notoriously difficult composition but infinitely worth the effort. To be captivated by Sibelius's Fifth (voted the favorite that year in Music 1) emboldened one to attack his Seventh, even though he had been very sneaky and written it all in one movement.

Vincent Morgan's legacy to us, may he rest in peace.

I competed for Glee Club and Choir my freshman year, and stuck with the Choir for three reasons, which I here list in ascending order of importance: (1) I came from a "minister's family," and singing sacred music didn't turn me off; (2) we had to go to required chapel anyhow, so why not go and sing; and (3) the job paid sixty dollars a year. Sixty dollars was a magnificent sum in the financially uncomplicated era of the late '30s.

But along the way I got more than the sixty dollars I had bargained for in the person of Henry Mishkin, a brand-new assistant professor of music, who directed the choir. With gentle strength he whipped us into an extraordinarily sensitive musical body. There weren't many religious types among us, but the sense of the holy really came through at a lot of Sunday afternoon required chapels that were redeemed by the anthems if not by the sermons.

"Papa" Mishkin (Bill Whiteside tacked that sobriquet on him after one particularly great Sunday) gave us the feeling that Bach was really pretty avant garde, and as a result we learned a whole treasure trove of Palestrina, di Lasso, William Byrd, and such. I don't know what Professor Mishkin's own religious inclinations were, or whether he had any particular sense of identification with Judaism, but he gave me a better feel for the mystery of the Christian story by the way he conducted passion music than I ever got subsequently from the professional obligation of reading many theologians' words about what is called the doctrine of the atonement.

We could always tell whether we had come through or not; he would place the yellow pencil with which he had been conducting (we were always going to get him an honest-to-God baton) back on the music rack of the organ, and give us a nod, usually containing *some* measure of approbation. There was one luminous occasion during a Palestrina *Ave Verum* when the look on his face was as close to what a beholder of the beatific vision must resemble, as anything I ever expect to see. During such high moments, he got out of us a degree of musical purity that provides a musical analogue to the ancient doctrine of transubstantiation: as the priest by grace can transform mere bread into Christ's presence, so Professor Mishkin (by grace as well?) was able to transform forty examples of rough-hewn secularity into almost pure sublimity.

On two other occasions, at least, the same thing happened. One was a winter offering of William Byrd's *I Will Not Leave Thee Comfortless,* so purely done that I have never wanted to hear it again for fear it would be a letdown. The other was a Christmas candlelight service when the Man-with-the-Yellow-Pencil drew from Bob McMullin an opening solo rendering of the words "Ava Maria" so effortless and soaring that it transported us to at least the third heaven (which is as far as Saint Paul ever got in this life) and left us singing from there for the rest of the service.

I'm not sure I have ever gotten all the way back down.

5 Love, Sex, and the Family
Challenges and Choices

When I was serving as chaplain on a navy troop transport during World War II, an approach to a port where members of the crew would have time ashore was sometimes preceded by what was called "a morality lecture." This event featured the chaplain and the ship's doctor, in that order. The chaplain, as the official custodian of morality, would give a brief talk about the ensuing shore leave that could be summarized by the word "don't." The doctor would then speak, and the gist of his comments usually was, "However, since you probably will, here are some precautions . . ."

Let me hasten to establish my turf before some retired Navy doctor calls for equal time. I offer comments in four areas: (1) a quick overview of the current scene; (2) some reflections on the social (and social justice) dimensions of love, sex, and "rules"; (3) pluses and minuses created by the intrusion of organized religion; and (4) half a dozen value-orientations we can share as we look to some rebuilding for the future.

The Current Scene

First, then, a reminder of the social context of the theme.

There is an idealized picture of love, sex, and the family that some of you may remember. It was epitomized by Ozzie and Harriet, "Leave It to Beaver," and innumerable Sunday school manuals on what were then chastely referred to as "boy and girl relationships."

Presented as the keynote address at the biannual meeting of the Association of Marriage and Family Therapists, Santa Clara County chapter, Stanford, California, October 1992.

The recipe for the mix went something like this: take two virgins, one of each sex, mix together thoroughly to produce an average of 2.3 children. Situate them in an attractive home in the suburbs, in which all the rooms are immaculate, and the cookie jar is always full. Place the father in a downtown office and give the mother control of the household (something that in those days was never defined as "work"). Have them attend church together on weekends (more likely Episcopal than Baptist). Permit small crises to arise from time to time, always resolved before the final commercial, in which the siblings accept the more mature wisdom of their parents. There is never even the hint of an "affair." What could they possibly desire that they don't already have?

We know that that world is not only gone, but gone for good. Even at its height, it described only a tiny sliver of the population—upwardly mobile, middle-class whites, very class-oriented.

Today, both parents have to work, and more and more couples are unable to find two jobs, let alone one. The cost of housing is so prohibitive that many of them will never own their own home. The husband's job is precarious: the firm has just announced that it will lay off seven thousand workers during the next fiscal year. With insecurity all over the place, wife beating and other kinds of physical violence are on the increase. For the children in such families, it is a statistical probability that by the early teens most of them will be sexually active, even though the high incidence of AIDS, along with the fences being built around abortion, take some of the thrill out of it. At least 10 percent of the population is gay or lesbian, and in some quarters this is still an awesome barrier to social acceptance. "Families" are more and more of a euphemism, increasingly dependent on a single parent, who in most cases will turn out to be the mother rather than the father. And the whole despairing structure is compounded by the easy accessibility of drugs and the overwhelming tendency to resort to them when things are too hot to handle.

Social Concerns and Social Justice Issues

We can get some leverage on dealing with this morass by examining some of the implications of the third term in our title, "family." This word has become politically charged, and we are on the receiving end of an endless barrage of comments and pronouncements about what is called "the recovery of family values." Pat Robertson gives an allegedly Protestant version of the theme, Pat Buchanan addresses himself to Catholics, while Dan Quayle picks up any remaining items.

For our present purposes, let the concept of "family" be invoked to underline an obvious though often overlooked point, which is that all aspects of human life — sex and love especially — are *communal in nature*. I do not mean just the fact that sex and love involve a community of two individuals, but the fact that these individuals, in their oneness, are inevitably in relation to other individuals, other couples, and other social groups, and cannot survive in isolation from many kinds and levels of community. This comes as a surprise to many teenagers, who assume that the terms of a presumably "private" relationship involve only the other partner. Having sex or not, for example, they interpret as nobody's business but theirs, a decision that affects only the two of them.

And this, of course, is stark unreality. If they marry, or enter into a long-time relationship, their dealings with their respective new families will have to be factored in. If they have children, a further vast arena of corporate relationships is opened up. If theirs is a same-sex relationship, there will be all kinds of public judgments, sometimes of approval but more likely of disapproval. If they transmit AIDS, another social network is created. If their commitment to one another is only casual, the long-term communal consequences may still be great, affecting their relationship with future sexual partners, running the risk that settling for momentary gratification will incrementally lessen the possibility of long-term commitments.

On another level, if violence or rape or ongoing exploitation persistently characterize the presumably "private" relationship, the society as a whole will claim a legitimate right to enter in to control the guilty partner. What we call "social injustice" becomes a component in what they may have originally imagined to be a strictly private relationship.

When we use the term "social justice," we usually mean decisions about whether to wage war or not, or how to restructure the economy in the direction of fairness. But issues such as child molestation, wife beating, failure to keep up-to-date on alimony payments, or ingesting drugs during pregnancy, are areas in which social justice concerns, community concerns, family concerns, and finally so-called "individual" concerns about sex and love all overlap.

Social justice has to do with issues, of power and regulating its abuse. If a family is falling apart because the father is putting in a seventy-hour week just to survive financially, the overall situation is rampant with *in*justice—the exploitation of the father by the corporation and the consequent harm done to wife and children, to take only one example. If both parents are forced to work for sheer economic survival, the children are victims of injustice, and principles of social justice must be invoked by adequate day-care centers, more generous maternity and paternity leave for parents, or whatever.

So questions of sex, love, marriage, family, and long-term relationships, whether heterosexual or homosexual, are not just individual private matters, but must be seen in relation to the whole social fabric of the whole human family.

Organized Religion

The intrusion of organized religion onto the scene has been a mixed blessing at best and a disaster at worst. James Nelson, one of our most astute Protestant thinkers, has summarized the traditional Christian confusion about sex and love as follows: "Sex is dirty; save it for someone you love." Especially since Augustine (who affirmed that marriages populate earth but virgins populate heaven), the Christian view has been ambiguous, with Christians suffering from hang-ups that Jews mercifully seem to have avoided. My own denomination officially declares quite lyrically that sex is a glorious gift of God, but immediately goes on to assert that ordination to proclaim the glorious gift is absolutely denied to those who are known to be gay or lesbian and unrepentant.

The received wisdom is encapsulated in the formula, "Abstinence before marriage, faithfulness within marriage, celibacy after marriage." Tough luck for everyone else. The view furnishes no good news to those who are unmarried, or divorced, or separated, or homosexual, or deprived by death of a marriage partner. The most that religion can offer them is a choice between guilt and frustration. If you do it you're sinful; if you don't do it, you go bonkers.

The fulcrum is almost always the discussion of marriages. In effect, anything goes within heterosexual marriage, nothing goes outside of such a marriage. While this is a tidy arrangement syllogistically, in human experience it is riddled with ambiguities. There can be rape in the marriage bed. There can be exploitation if love has disappeared from the marriage, and sex as physical gratification alone has replaced sex as an expression of love. Some sexual relationships outside of marriage are more tender and more true than a great deal that goes on within marriage simply because a marriage certificate has been signed.

But the minute one begins to talk that way, the boom is lowered. It is charged that such an outlook will lead to permissiveness, promiscuity, the breakdown of marriage, and the destruction of "family values," not to mention the certain decline and fall of Western civilization. No standards will be left. Only moral chaos will remain. I will return to that viewpoint in a moment, but before doing so I want to raise three specific issues where the contribution of religion is murky and often destructive.

The first two of these are incorporated in the never-ending controversy over *abortion and birth control*. I will not rehearse the arguments pro and con—that would be sufficient for a whole book in itself. I will only say that in discussion of abortion the tone is so strident, and the participants on both sides so rigid, that significant dialogue is virtually impossible. There are moral questions concerning abortion that deserve discussion, and they do not get it, because the participants generate heat rather than light, anger rather than understanding. At the moment, I think our most significant contribution will consist in trying simply to make the rules of exchange more humane.

Controversy over *birth control* is very different. I do not believe that the arguments against birth control come close to being convincing, and the evidence is clear that a great majority of Roman Catholic couples share that conviction and ignore the official teaching of their church. This is largely an internal Catholic issue, and the rest of us will not contribute significantly to its resolution. The Roman Catholic Church seldom repudiates past doctrinal positions, but it does frequently diminish the attention given to certain of them. (Who today takes seriously the medieval doctrine of "the two swords"?) If similar subordination on the issue of birth control were to take place in the church, as I believe it will, it would have the important social consequence that the number of conceptions would drop significantly due to the use of birth control, and this would in turn dramatically reduce the number of instances where abortion even needed to be contemplated.

Another clash between most church teaching and the social reality occurs over the question of *homosexuality*. The furthest most churches will go is to say that God loves homosexuals despite their deviance, and so Christians must love them too, even while praying vigorously for their conversion — a demeaning conclusion to an unworthy argument.

A major part of the controversy centers on ordination to ministry. I have considerable personal investment in this controversy, namely the number of gay and lesbian students I have had in at least two decades of seminary teaching. They experience an authentic call to ministry, and in the face of that are almost uniformly told by their church bodies, "If you want to be ordained, there is only one way: lie. Don't tell us you are homosexual and we will ordain you. But if you tell us the truth about who you are, we will refuse your request."

This invidious exercise of church leadership is hardly a rousing invitation to gays and lesbians to become part of the body of Christ. The good news is that increasing numbers of congregations are beginning to defy the norm and offer invitations to membership and ordination without strings attached. That is where the hope lies. But it is still a dreary picture. Another, more fortunate, side to the church's engagement with sexual issues is slowly gaining currency in some church circles, though in all honesty I must report that it is still vehemently rejected by the majority of my Presbyterian colleagues. That fact, however, only increases my reportorial zeal.

One begins by repudiating an ethic that is purely legalistic, that is, with rules that are clear and unyielding and nonnegotiable. The favorite one goes: the only appropriate exercise of sex is within marriage, which incidentally limits the possibility of sex to about 31 percent of the denomination. What about the other 69 percent: singles, divorced people, homosexuals, young people, and so on? Officially, heroic self-denial is their only option.

How do we move beyond that? By noting, first of all, that the criterion of marriage is no necessary assurance of the presence of creative sexual love. As already noted, there is much exploitation within marriage: patriarchy, violence, coldness, rape. This doesn't mean marriage is not a good thing, but it does mean that it is not *automatically* a good thing.

Is there, then, a criterion other than marriage to test the appropriateness or inappropriateness of sexual love between two persons? A rejected Presbyterian report (Keeping Body and Soul Together: Sexuality, Spirituality and Social Justice, 203rd General Assembly, 1991) says yes. It is the criterion of *justice/love*. The presence of both justice and love is essential to a relationship, especially one that includes sexual relations. Justice alone can be harsh, and love alone can be sentimental, and that being so, both are needed in a full human relationship if it is not to founder. Exploitation is ruled out by this criterion; so is domination. Love (and not just infatuation) must be present. Justice (and not just meeting legalistic requirements) must be present. Some marriages would meet the test of justice/love, others would not. Similarly, some unmarried relationships would meet the test, others would not.

It is important to notice, in proposing such a standard, that rather than fostering permissiveness (as many people fear), it would create a *more,* rather than a less, demanding ethic. Its criteria are not easy to meet.

These are only the broad strokes of a position that needs much ongoing exploration. And I must add that I am personally an enthusiastic practitioner of heterosexual marriage, and take the criterion of justice/love seriously. But that does not entitle me to legislate for those who are not married, by choice or circumstance. And I rejoice when, in those other circumstances, relationships based on justice/love are possible for them too.

Toward New Understanding

So far, I have been giving a report. But I want now to shift gears and explore whether out of the above discussion we can discern fresh pointers toward a new understanding of love, sex, and the family. I will very briefly describe half a dozen value-concerns that I believe most readers of a book like this one could affirm and share, whatever our individual religious or nonreligious orientations may be.

1. Many of the traditions represented by most readers of this book affirm that there is *a sense of mystery or wonder* in the face of the world we inhabit. We can't put it all together and understand it by a series of logical propositions, but we can affirm that there is something about this creation that finally leaves us awestruck, whether it is beauty, the presence of love, the immensity of space, the mystery of time, or whatever. (To be sure, we may also be outraged by what we see and cry out against it, but even that cry is an implicit recognition that things ought to be different from what they are.) Gabriel Marcel reminds us that the universe does not confront us as a problem to be solved, as though full understanding were just around the corner, but rather as *a mystery to be lived,* an invitation to participate in something the full meaning of which eludes us, but the worthwhileness of which attracts us.

I suggest that it is this attitude of mystery and wonder that we need to bring to a new understanding of sex and love—neither of which can be codified and ranked and manipulated but both of which remain wonderful mysteries into which we can enter and which, even though we will never fully understand them, are realities for which we can be infinitely grateful. In this age of clinical sex, for example, when all can be seen and exploited on wide-screen TV, the wonder is no longer present. Sex has been reduced to gymnastics for two. It has become ordinary. Let us recapture its wonder.

2. A second thing is very clear, and has previously been noted: *there is a social dimension to being an individual.* We do not exist in solitariness; we exist always in the context of a world and especially in the context of other people. We are initially totally dependent on them, and must gradually wean ourselves away, not to find fulfillment in a new isolation, but in ever-widening circles of community—the family, the school, the business world, the relationship to another person out of which new persons are created, on and on and on. In everything we do, we bump into, or make way

for, others. The worst punishment society can inflict short of death is solitary confinement.

What we do has social consequences. The very act of sex is the most firm—and wonderful—underlining of our communal nature. Not only are we affected, but we affect someone else, for good or for ill, but never for naught.

3. The other side of being a social creature is to be an individual creature, and not only that but an *individual creature endowed with infinite worth,* never to be exploited or "used" as an object. Different traditions define this uniqueness in different ways: Quakers talk about "that of God" or even "the seed of God" within everyone. Jews and Christians talk about being made in "the image of God," described lyrically as being "little lower than God." Others seek to embody the indwelling spirit of the Buddha.

People often assume that the basic reality is the individual, and that when there are enough individuals around they will somehow create community. But I want to insist that from the beginning we are part of a community, and that it is only as we live within community that our individuality can mature and more clearly define who we are. The Hebrew scriptures underline this point by affirming that God does not first call Moses or Abraham or Deborah, and then place them in a community; rather, God first of all calls into being a community—Israel—into which Moses and Abraham and Deborah are placed, and only out of which do they emerge as distinct individuals of infinite worth.

Surely this sense of the infinite worth of the "other" is a crucial part of any true understanding of love and sex. Love and sex go astray to just the degree that we try to reduce the worth of the other to something that can be manipulated or managed or "used" for our gratification or the expense of the other. To see the other as of infinite worth is to begin to see that all persons must be accorded that high estimate.

4. As persons, we are able to have a measure of control over our lives. However much we may abuse it, "freedom" to some degree defines who we are. But we simultaneously have to recognize that we are *not* free to do any damn thing we please. *Our freedom has some constraints built into it,*

and no matter how unhappy that makes us, there is no way we can function without acknowledging and respecting those constraints. If we fail to do so, we bring about our own destruction and probably the destruction of others. For the most part we don't invent the constraints—they are "there," and we ignore them at our peril. We live in a world where we don't make up all the rules.

This can be stated in another way: *we live in a moral universe.* I feel less secure with this language, since we find so much in our universe that seems amoral if not immoral, and that needs to be challenged rather than accepted in some kind of metaphysical grab bag. At the very least, however, the things we do have consequences, and it is part of our responsibility as moral beings to measure those consequences.

If we take the reality of constraints seriously, this may not give us a lot of specific guidance about love and sex and family, but it will set the context within which to reach for some new guidelines, and in the area of sex and love, we gradually learn, often the hard way, what the constraints and the liberations are. I submit that we cannot indefinitely "use" other people for our own gratification at the expense of theirs, without things beginning to unravel. We can share our vulnerability with each other, and discover that both of us are strengthened thereby. We cannot be sexually promiscuous without the possibility of becoming infected and of infecting others. We can put the good of the other ahead of our own good, and find that doing so in itself becomes a good. We must acknowledge constraints.

5. Whatever we know about the order of things—the possibility of a moral universe, the objective reality of constraints around our freedom, the quality of life in community, and so on—we discover to our initial surprise that these extraordinary things come to us in *very ordinary ways,* through the stuff of everyday experience. We don't have to go to mountaintops for illumination, even though that may help some people. Many religious traditions, for example, have a ceremony of eating and drinking—very mundane, down-to-earth stuff—and as a result participants feel themselves indwelt by God. In Eastern Orthodoxy and some forms of Catholicism, the ordinary act of smelling—in this case, incense—puts one in touch with ul-

timate mystery. Jews look at the ordinary, mundane world and see it as God's handiwork. From this perspective, there is no separate sacred realm to be achieved only by forsaking the ordinary secular realm.

And this, too, helps us to rethink an approach to love, sex, and family. Love between two humans beings is not only a good thing in itself, but can be a means through which one is put in touch with the love of God for both persons as well. God is not just "out there," but in the very heart of human intimacy. If that language sounds too forbidding, let us simply say that if there *is* a divine love to be experienced, it will be experienced in the midst of human life and not somewhere separated from human life. We cannot separate the sacred from the secular, the spiritual from the physical. "Carnal experience" is a pointer to God.

In the creation myth in Genesis, after each day of creation (of the firmament, the sun, the stars, and so on) there is the refrain "And God saw that it was good." But after the sixth day, which included the creation of male and female, the creation of sex, the refrain goes, "And God saw that it was *very* good." We are not doing justice to our subject matter of love, sex, and family until we recognize that in addition to all their inherent worth those realities are pointers to all that is most creative—and good.

6. Finally, every religious heritage offers something that can only be described by such a word as *grace*. Grace is another way of talking about love, but a special kind of love—love that is undeserved but is given anyhow, and sustains even when it might seem ready to issue rebuff. At its best, it characterizes the love between two people, both of whom realize that by no stretch of the imagination do they "deserve" each other, and who yet continue to receive something they cannot earn. It is all gift, sheer gift, for which, rather than preening ourselves at how good we are, we can only feel and try to express gratitude.

And to carry our previous point further, this experience of human love—undeserved but given anyhow—is likewise a way of talking about divine love, whatever words we use. In the experience of the race, human love and divine love are somehow mutually illuminated by one another. This is not a point at which everyone arrives, but it is always a possibility for those who seek it and those who cherish it.

Grace, then, means both forgiveness and empowerment. We fail, and instead of being clobbered we are forgiven and given a new start. Forgiveness thus becomes a source of empowerment. We are not trapped in the past. We have more going for us than we realized — the support of another, the wiping out of guilt, a brand-new beginning. Surely there is no better context for making something new and creative out of love, sex, and family.

6 Memory
A Three-Sided Virtue

On a gray November night in 1963, I was well launched into a lecture on "religious liberty" at the Canadian Theological College in Rome, when Cardinal Léger interrupted the session to inform us that John F. Kennedy had been shot and was not expected to live. The meeting was transformed into a time of intercession for the president's life, which, as we later learned, was already beyond the power of intercessory prayer.

We Americans attending the Vatican Council began to hear from our families back home about the national mood after the tragedy: strangers in the streets hugging each other amid tears; radio and TV stations excising commercials and playing classical music, people entering churches for the first time in decades, shared numbness and muted rage. We soon realized that we had missed forever an important national sharing of grief and outrage and purification, for the simple reason that *we were not there.* Those present had experiences—something they could only partially describe to us, something we could never experience in its fullness . . .

On a bright July day in 1934, Duncan Mackay and I got up early, and made it, two fourteen-year-olds unencumbered by adults, to the Polo Grounds to attend the All-Star Game, a national liturgical event, then still in its infancy.

We were richly rewarded. Giants pitcher Carl Hubbell, *consecutively* struck out the five most-feared sluggers in the American League: Babe Ruth, Lou Gehrig, Jimmy Foxx, Al Simmons,

Originally published in *Christianity and Crisis* (February 1989). Used by permission.

and Joe Cronin. Carl Hubbell died in 1988, and this game was mentioned most frequently in the obituaries. I read them with a thrill of excitement: *we were there.* We saw it happen. *We remember it.* (Because I was there I also remember something none of the obituaries mentioned: In his final inning, Carl Hubbell also struck out Lefty Gomez, an event the non-afficionados thought incidental, since Gomez's lifetime batting average hovered in the neighborhood of .091. But in the record books a strikeout is a strikeout is a strikeout.)

Reflecting on these two episodes, I am struck by three of the characteristics of memory.

1. Most of all, *memory is communal.* When Kennedy died, the folks back home shared their grief with one another. All the events they described to us involved other people, often strangers, with whom they were bound together in a community defined by shock and need. I can be part of that community, part of that national memory, *but only by adoption,* as those who were there help me to enter part way, but only part way, with them.

Duncan Mackay and I have a shared memory, along with the 35,371 other people who were at the Polo Grounds with us. Were I to encounter one of those 35,371 fans today, we would have an instant rapport denied to other folk, however different our tastes or commitments in other areas of life turned out to be. But I am quite willing (perhaps too willing, my friends might say) to share those three spectacular innings when Carl Hubbell etched his name in eternity, so that they too can get a "feel" for what it was like to be there. We can give each other memories by proxy, but only by proxy.

To remember, then, means more than just to recall. As Wendell Berry reminds us in his novel *Remembering* (San Francisco: North Point Press, 1988), it also means to be re-membered (the opposite of being dismembered), to be drawn into a group or a circle from which we had, for whatever reasons, found ourselves excluded. Remembering means entering the member-ship of a community.

2. *Memory is selective.* That's the pitfall and the greatness. Yes, we readjust our memories in ways more convenient to our egos than the facts

would warrant, and we block out memories too painful to live with. But the greatness is that we can nurture other memories, cultivate them, live with them ever before us, and so let them help to redefine who we are. It works both ways. Some people actually welcomed Kennedy's death. That's hard for me to remember. And certain memories of him are not appealing. We subordinate them to the more creative ones. Now and then, but not often, Carl Hubbell got knocked out of the box in the first inning, but I choose to remember the first three innings of the All-Star Game as normative.

Right now we are still exercising our selective memories in relation to the Reagan and Bush years. What events should we remember? It all depends on the perspective we bring *to* those years. Do those years represent new opportunities for peace (Gorbachev, treaties, summit meetings) or to corruptions of power (Grenada, support for the contras, lack of support for the homeless)? Probably a little of both, and we can have it any way we want it. With so many events to choose from, selective retention is necessary for brains capable of absorbing only finite amounts of information.

3. For this reason, *memory is a challenge*. The payoff is whether we use our selected memories for good or ill. The selective memory of Nazis concentrating on past German glory energized the dream of a Third Reich that would last a thousand years.

The selective memory of Jews, for whom the Nazi dream was an anti-Semitic nightmare, was energized by their determination to survive in order to bear witness. The devastating memories of the death camps have been used by survivors not to purvey hatred (which would have been a totally understandable reaction) but to tell the story and imbed it in *our* memories (as much as possible for those who weren't there) so that the world will hear the message of "Never again": never again genocide, never again torture, never again the burning of children.

For a somewhat similar reason, I want Americans to remember the worlds of Ronald Reagan and George Bush just before leaving office, and our widely accepted axioms that the homeless are homeless because they choose to be so, and that they sleep over grates in the downtown areas of our cities because they prefer to be there. I want such words remembered, not to pillory individuals, but to call to mind and demonstrate the insensitivity of so many of us in the face of widespread injustices to many of our number. We Americans often thrive on the ease and convenience of solving problems by denying their existence, thereby relieving us of the need to do anything about them. The memory of such attitudes can be a catalyst warning to us not to decide that those who suffer are not really suffering, and not to accept a scheme of things in which the needs of the poor can be ignored with ostrichlike evasion.

At its best, the church embodies these three understandings of memory. The church has a *communal* memory that we call "the good news," that remembers all who respond to it; the church fine-tunes that message by a high degree of *selectivity,* proclaiming that certain events clustered around Jesus of Nazareth are the important events to remember and live by; and the church *challenges* us to put those selected memories to work, in order to create a world in which peace and justice are not only the content of angels' songs to shepherds but marching orders for the rest of us.

Part 2.
Religion and Politics, Religion as Politics

To some readers, this section, reacquainting us with idols and evil, may seem too strident, at best speaking out of a situation that now lies behind us. To other readers the word "dated" might seem appropriate (as in "dated and therefore of little current concern").

I would argue that such sentiments are inappropriate. It has been precisely to *retain* the context of this section that shrillness occasionally abounds. All of which helps to flesh out the theme of "speaking of Christianity," in that it implies that the whole range of Christian thought is appropriate for examination. Those of us from comfortable surroundings need to be reminded that all that has really changed in our lifetimes is that very little has changed except for the worse. Things today are only more subtle versions of what came before. Torture continues, but is slightly more hidden—though not always. Duplicity in high places remains, as every election, including the most recent, reminds us. We have much to learn from the past.

My thesis is that the stridency must remain or we will fail to hear what the past tells us. So, we deal with Christianity and idols, Christianity and betrayal, Christianity and ruthlessness, Christianity and demonic tyrants—

but also with Christianity and justice, Christianity and compassion, Christianity and hope, and first and last, Christianity and politics.

All the chapters in Part 2 revolve around the hinge of politics, though my ultimate dependency is on the Bible, which turns out to be not only a useful interpretive tool but the most demanding, upsetting, and radical political tract the world has ever had to confront.

Check it out.

As for moving from past to future, maybe the best thing that could happen would be for us to start asking the question that heads chapter 11, "Can we have a just and compassionate society?"

7 The Bible Acquaints Us with Idols

When a stranger comes up to you smiling, asks your opinion about breaking the law in the name of conscience, and displays great interest in what your local church is doing specifically and in who is involved, think before you answer. The questioner may be someone whom your tax dollars are helping to support, and who is playing the role of hypocrite, that is, wearing a mask and representing himself or herself as the opposite of who he or she truly is. For our government has adopted a favorite device of totalitarian nations. It pretends to be sympathetic, while infiltrating your group. If you are not careful, you can put those with whom you are associated behind bars, and they might even have a place there for you.

Why is there a conflict between religion and the state, so that the above paragraph should be taken seriously? The answer to the question is contained in the theme of this chapter: biblical concepts of idolatry, the worship of idols or false gods. If we define "God" as the one to whom we give our ultimate allegiance, the one who commands our final loyalty when the chips are down, then the conflict is clear. On the one side is the God to whom we are trying to give allegiance, the God who sides with the poor and dispossessed, the God who is the God of justice and compassion, the God who bids us likewise to align ourselves with the victims rather than the victimizers, the God of the Hebrew and Christian scriptures.

Originally presented at a symposium on "Sanctuary" in Phoenix, Arizona, January 1975; published in *Sanctuary*, ed. Gary MacEoin (New York: Harper & Row, 1985), 55–61. Used by permission.

On the other side is the god of those who infiltrate into our midst to seek our arrest and imprisonment, the god of the state.

We are now being told not to oppose what the state is doing, and are warned that if we do not give uncritical allegiance to the state it will "get" us. Salvadorans have been fleeing from El Salvador for years, because the Salvadoran government, supported by *our* government, has been repressive and has killed those who challenge it—more than seventy thousand deaths so far, mostly of peasants, until the recent establishment of a tenuous "peace." A group of North Americans has been trying to help the refugees, assisting their arrival in ways our government until quite recently has deemed illegal. For many years almost all Salvadoran refugees were routinely shipped back home where they became candidates for murder, since our government claimed that they were only "political" refugees and not entitled to our protection.

This has been an act of calculated callousness on the part of our government. And when, in the name of all that is decent and humane, U.S. citizens began to say no to this activity by our government, and tried to counter it, they in turn were spied upon, informed upon, rounded up, indicted, and forced to stand trial. We need to remember what they, too, have suffered.

It may be, as the Bible says, a fearful thing to fall into the hands of the living God. It is also a fearful thing to fall into the hands of a false god, an idol, a human construct, telling us, "Don't cross my will, don't defy us, don't disagree, for if you do, we will find ways to get rid of you and to get rid of the people you are trying so mistakenly to help."

So the question becomes, very simply, Which God do we serve? The living God or an idol, the God of the Bible or the god of the state?

We have already learned some things about this god of the state from the Hebrew Bible, and its powerful portrayal of evil. The same God is present, under only slightly different guise, in the Christian scriptures as well, which pick up on the major themes of the Jewish scriptures on this matter. The demand is the same: "You shall have no other gods before me." The theme and its mode of presentation are worth some reflection.

In the early church the most basic Christian confession of faith was only two words long. (As a theologian who has had a professional obligation to wade through endlessly long creeds and confessions, I have often wished that subsequent Christians had been as economical as their forebears were in their use of words. The confession went *Kurios Christos,* meaning "Christ is *Kurios* or Lord." *Kurios* is the Greek word for that to which ultimate allegiance is given. "Who is your *Kurios?*" early Christians would be asked. The response for them was clear, "The *Christos,* Jesus of Nazareah." That response at first sounds purely theological, able to engender heated discussion about such things as the relative merits of docetism or modalistic Monarchianism, as well as a cause of endless painful controversy between Christians and Jews.

Let us remember, however, that *it was a political statement as well.* In the Roman Empire at that time every citizen had to make an annual public declaration of allegiance to the empire. The declaration went *Kurios Caesar,* meaning "Caesar (the state) is *kurios,* is Lord." Caesar is the one to whom you must give your ultimate allegiance. So if, instead, you were so rash as to make the theological statement *Kurios Christos,* Christ is the object of my ultimate allegiance, you would also be making a very political statement indeed. You were announcing not only your primary and ultimate loyalty to *Christos,* but at best only secondary and subordinate loyalty to Caesar.

Press the logic. Since Christ is Lord, you were saying, Caesar is not Lord. Caesar is a pretender to the title of Lord. To affirm Caesar as Lord would be to affirm allegiance to a false god, an idol.

Caesars don't like that one bit, whether they reside in Rome or in Washington. So the First Commandment, "You shall have no other gods before me," and the earliest Christian confession, "Christ is Lord," are making the same claim in different language, a claim around which all of us not only can, but must, rally. In the name of saying yes to what is ultimate for us, we must be prepared to say no to whatever falsely claims that place of ultimacy. To say yes to the true God is to say no to the idols, wherever and whatever they are.

Many times the voice of that idol today is the voice of the contemporary caesar, our own government, which is telling us, "We decree that you must turn your backs on refugees, those who are fleeing from the modern pharaohs in their own lands. We decree that you grant them no sanctuary, allow them no place to lay their heads, and return them, if it comes to that, to firing squads."

If we ask why, our government functionaries have an answer: "We have decided that they are not wanted here. We have decided in advance that their claims are spurious. We have decided that they are only trying to take advantage of us. Besides, if we were to grant them refuge, we would be conceding that their government, which we support, is an evil government, which we cannot afford to do. So act in accord with us, or we will make it mighty tough for you."

So our government has decided that we who feel strongly about the need to provide sanctuary shall not be allowed to provide it. Our consciences are to be made hostage to repressive measures, against suffering people, by our own government. And we really have no choice but to say no to all that. And many are already paying a heavy price.

If the rest of us take seriously the biblical call to oppose idolatry wherever it breaks out—especially when it breaks out among those close to home—we have no choice but single-mindedly to stand with them and give them our very public help and support. To the degree that we are impeded from carrying out the work they have begun, we must take their places and continue their work. We must ensure that what they have been about becomes what we continue to be about.

There is nothing our government would like better than to have that agenda fail, to have us become fearful and divided, or to start dissipating our energies in a dozen different directions. To the degree that we allow ourselves to be intimidated by this action of the government, we too will be worshiping false gods; we too will be succumbing to the wiles of the modern pharaoh, the contemporary caesar, who this time—let us be clear—is likely to reside in Washington.

Let us remember the frightening analogue to what we are confronting today, the risk, not so long ago, of the Nazi state and its increasingly persistent attempts to get rid of the Jews. If we had been in Germany in the 1930s and a Jew had come to us and asked to be hidden because otherwise he or she might die at the hands of a hostile government, we would all like to believe that we would have helped the fleeing person. The fact is, of course, that Christians had an abysmal record in that situation. With very few exceptions, everybody caved in, and the state was able to carry out its policies with little resistance.

Translate the question from the 1930s to the present time. If we are Americans in the 1980s and 1990s, and Salvadorans and Guatamalans come to us and ask to be hidden, because otherwise they might die at the hands of a hostile government, will we take them in? To the degree that people in Germany failed to give sanctuary and hiding to Jews, to that degree the power of the Nazi government increased and became more repressive. To the degree that people in the United States fail to give sanctuary and housing to Salvadorans and Guatemalans, knuckling under to the tactics now being displayed by our government, to that degree the power of our government to become increasingly repressive will be enhanced, and the lives of Salvadorans and Guatemalans even further jeopardized.

We Christians failed the Jews in the 1930s, and we have unfinished business with the Jewish community on that score. But let us at least salvage out of that tragic failure a determination that we will not fail Salvadorans and Guatemalans now. The responsibility is inescapable.

Yes, there is a conflict between religion and the state today. Yes, idolatry in the biblical sense is alive and well, flourishing in our midst. To those realities there can be only one response. We must expand our efforts on behalf of the victims, lest, by failing to do so, we betray the victims and become accomplices of the victimizers.

8 Religion and the Role of Dissent

Religion plays many roles in our lives. To some it gives *a sense of meaning;* there is a purpose to life even when it is hard to discern, and when we can't discern it, at least we can proceed on the assumption that somehow it will all be made clear. To others it provides *strength in time of testing;* we are forced into a role that is unpopular, but we have the reassurance that whoever the foes lined up against us, the divine resources of power are available to us in withstanding them. To others religion offers *comfort in the midst of sorrow;* life falls apart but we are reassured that, in the biblical imagery, "underneath are the everlasting arms," and they will hold us up. To others, alas, religion seems to do little more than *lay on a guilt trip;* whatever we do, there always seems to be more that we were supposed to do.

But beyond these (and many other) things, religion does something else. It provides a norm, a standard, *by which we are rendered dissatisfied with the way things are*—not in such a way as simply to immobilize us with guilt but as a way of liberating us for change. It gives us something we can affirm, say yes to, in the name of which we can say no to certain things in our personal lives, or in society as a whole, that need to be challenged.

If the norm that religion supplies is, for instance, justice, then in the name of a God of justice we have to say no to injustice by seeking to eradicate it. If the norm is love, then in the name of commitment to a God of love we must challenge acts of lovelessness. Religion so conceived can be a potent source of dissent,

Excerpts from the Eugene M. Burke Lectureship on Religion and Society, delivered in San Diego, May 1, 1986.

a platform from which to determine what we must affirm and what we must disavow in our individual and corporate lives.

I can sum up both the greatness and the demonry of this conviction by sharing the statement of an anonymous seventeenth-century writer: "I had rather see coming toward me a whole regiment with drawn swords, than one lone Calvinist convinced that he is doing the will of God." The greatness of the position is that one who feels that he or she is doing God's will is liberated from all kinds of fears, can rise to new heights of courage, and occasionally rise to stem the tide of what might be evil. The demonry, of course, is that it is far too easy, and not only for Calvinists, to become persuaded that what they want to do, and what God wants them to do, are identical. And that is the point at which dissent within the body politic and dissent within ecclesiastical bodies have quite similar goals.

Let us proceed on the assumption that dissent is an important part of American life — an assumption concerning which I do not anticipate much dissent. That is what the democratic process is all about. Yet whenever in our national life people begin to fear some outside force, some enemy, dissent becomes a potential casualty, progressively equated with lack of patriotism, disloyalty, and (if the times are bad enough) treason. Many will remember when a Democratic administration accused those who were against the Vietnam War of being anti-American and pro-communist, in addition to being woolly-headed dupes. Those of the present generation will remember that within recent times a Republican administration has accused those who are against funding right-wing regimes of being anti-American and pro-communist, even when the genial part of the charge (being woolly-headed dupes) has disappeared from the indictment. I cite the two examples deliberately, to indicate that neither political party has a monopoly on name calling when its own policies are being challenged in the public arena.

Now against that kind of hysteria (for I believe that is what it is) I want to set the counter-assumption that *dissent is a very important act of loyalty*. Dissenters against this or that policy are saying, in effect, "We must judge our country not by what it presently is, but by what it ought to be — and when there is a discrepancy between the two, it is an act of true patriotism

47

to point it out. If the vision is 'liberty and justice for all,' that means *all*, and not just for folks like us, who tend on the whole to be white and middle class."

The usual way to express our dissent is through the electoral process. Sometimes that doesn't work or is perceived by dissenters as not working rapidly enough. In the '60s, for example, American blacks came to the conclusion (quite rightly, as we now see) that the process *wasn't* working fast enough, and so blacks upped the ante for change by engaging in nonviolent civil disobedience, as a way to register urgent concern that the national theme was not just liberty and justice for whites, but for blacks as well. The dissenters took exception to laws, usually local ordinances, that denied them equal access to restaurants, hotels, and travel facilities, and appealed beyond local and state laws to federal laws, and—in this instance in particular—to a higher law, the law of God.

At this point, religion clearly enters into the discussion. To claim belief in a god is to proclaim an ultimate loyalty, whoever or whatever the "god" may be. It may be the God of the Bible, or the god equated with the state (nationalism is a particularly pervasive "god" in our day) or the god of nature, but whatever or whoever is the object of faith, the one making the faith claim is saying, "This comes first. Here is my highest loyalty."

It follows that the *nature* of the god in whom one believes will have important consequences for how one behaves. If you claim to believe in a nondiscriminatory god (a god, let us say, who does not give favors to white-skinned people that are denied to dark-skinned people), then you have a problem. Either you have to deny your belief in the nondiscriminatory god; or, in the name of that god, you have to challenge the discriminatory society by seeking to change it. You have no choice but to *dissent* from its customs and mores, and maybe even from its laws. Catholics in the Philippines came to this same conclusion. If they believed in justice, they couldn't support Marcos. If they believed in Marcos, they couldn't have justice. And so justice had to be chosen instead of Marcos. A clear-cut choice. And more honor, I say, to the people like Roman Catholic Cardinal Jaime Sin, who refused to equivocate or encourage the church to play a "neutral" role. He recognized that when it came to choosing between justice and injustice, there is no "neutral" position. If you try to be neutral you end up supporting injustice.

When we have to begin to choose between God and caesar, caesar becomes very unhappy. And most of the pressures in our public life are pressures to say yes to caesar. "Don't be different," we are counseled, "go along with the crowd. What make you think you have an inside track denied to the rest of us?" And if we persist in raising questions, the rhetoric of opposition is likely to be raised as well: "What are you, some kind of commy nut or something?" Some conservatives may put it in a little more genteel language, but not much.

Why does the issue so inflame the people on both sides? I think it is because both sides realize that the discussion cuts very close to the bone. The Hebrew prophets have given us the clue in this. For them, the great sin is not to disbelieve in God, the great sin is to believe in the wrong God. They have a word for this, and it is a word that is very relevant to our own situation. The sin that they most roundly condemn is *idolatry,* the worship of "idols," by which they mean false gods. And a choice must be made: either worship the true God, or you are, whether you know it or not, worshiping a false god.

If this sounds quaint and out-of-date, wait a moment; it is not old-fashioned, and it is not primitive. The New Testament, for example, picking up on this fundamental insight of the Hebrew scriptures, talks about idols too—the idolatry of money, the idolatry of law, and the idolatry of oppressive political power—and I submit that it would be hard to find more appealing candidates in the modern world than those three for taking the place of the God of the Bible: money, law and order, totalitarianism. When you make any one of those the number-one concern, you are worshiping an idol, and you need to be called to account. In different form, they may legitimately occupy subordinate roles: we need *some* money to survive, society must have *some* laws to survive, and *some* forms of government are legitimate. But the problem becomes acute when the idols won't occupy "subordinate roles" but insist on being center stage. And that, it seems to me, is where we are now in our national life, for whenever a government begins to question the legitimacy of dissent, and to equate dissent with

49

disloyalty, then the warning flags are up and we have to join the issue as clearly as we can. For we cannot "render to caesar" the uncritical loyalty and unquestioning support that caesar wants. For if we do that, we make caesar into God, and rule number one for any religion is that you cannot elevate to the status of God that which is not God.

Let us briefly examine one other biblical incident to nail down the point. I indicated earlier that it is *the nature of the God we believe in* that determines how we act in response to God. If our deity is malevolent, we can practice evil; if our God is unconcerned about the world, we can be unconcerned as well; if our God shows partiality to the white race, we can stomp on blacks. When we ask, "What is the nature of the God whom we have inherited from our own religious past?" there is no better place to turn for an answer than to the episode recorded in Exodus 20. The Israelites have made it out of Egypt and are beyond the clutches of the pharaoh, a demonic tyrant. They need some guidance, and Moses, you will remember, goes up Mount Sinai to get it. The result is a series of marching orders—ten, in all—that indicate pretty clearly how they are to comport themselves in relation to such nitty-gritty matters as sexual relations and private property. But before the marching order, God engages in a kind of act of self-definition, laying out the divine credentials, so to speak. There are no "proofs of God's existence" offered, no long list of philosophical or theological attributes, no clever dictionary definitions. There is one thing only, and it goes: "I am the Lord your God, who brought you out of the land of Egypt, out of the house of bondage" (Exodus 20:2). That's all. That, presumably, is sufficient.

And notice what it tells us. God is saying in effect: "Here is the kind of God I am. When you were in trouble, I came to your rescue. I helped you get your act together so that you could oppose Pharaoh and make your getaway. You were in the midst of an unjust situation and I intervened to put an end to the injustice. I am *the God of justice*. Justice is my middle name."

Having cleared the decks in such tidy fashion, God then gives the first of the marching orders, and it implicitly contains all the other nine. It, too, is a model of brevity. It goes: "You shall have no other gods before me." That's a way of saying, "Since I am a God of justice, you can never acquiesce to injustice. To let injustice flourish is to deny me, it is to *have* 'another god before me.' Since justice is at the top of my agenda, it had better be at the top of yours too."

That, I submit, gives us the stuff out of which we can begin to develop quite a bit of content about what such a God asks of us. We are to work for justice, and to combat injustice. We are to affirm those structures, convictions, and policies that extend justice, and challenge those structures, convictions, and policies that deny justice and extend injustice—and here is where the dissent comes in. We will still have lots of room to disagree about specifics (for example, which policies "enhance justice"?), but we will not be quite so much in the dark, for we will have a basis around which to debate those disagreements.

I stress this point because I do not want to claim that dissent is the prerogative of only certain groups in society, the special vocation, let us say, of the left rather than the right. It is the obligation of persons in every segment of society to raise warning voices when they see a conflict between what they believe is just, and what they perceive society or their government is doing. I take it to be the great virtue of democracy that the public arena is the place where we can debate such matters. And our criterion of justice furnishes a splendid point of intersection with our national life, one of the avowed aims of which is "liberty and *justice* for all."

9 A Protestant View of Justice

I am not going to start this chapter with a definition of justice, which is not a concept easily carved in stone. I am, however, helped by a comment once made by John Bennett, one of our most distinguished Protestant ethicists, that justice is seeing to it that every child gets his or her due. A society that gives priority to the needs of children will come close to being a just society. There was a wonderful phrase in the Chilean liberation struggle that captured this: *Y los únicos privilegiados seran los niños* (The only privileged ones will be the children).

Not only do children provide a creative focus for our initial concerns, they provide us with an important insight to further framing of the issue. Whenever we have to adjudicate quarrels between children, we discover that no matter how Solomonic our bottom line of appeal, the aggrieved child will almost invariably reply, "But that's not *fair!*" They did not discover this criterion of "fairness" by reading Aristotle or even John Bennett. And it seems to be built into us as adults that, especially when we are wronged, or upset by wrongdoing done to others, we remain true to the childhood reflex, "That's not fair!"

If I were to present this starting point in more sophisticated fashion, I believe it could be used as a basis for the traditional doctrine of "natural law," the conviction that even in a relatively fallen state, human beings retain some sense of right versus

Presented as the initial portion of a lecture given in the summer of 1994 at an international conference of Christians and Jews in Warsaw, Poland, and also to an ecumenical gathering at St. Mary's Cathedral in San Francisco, California, that same year. Published in an amended version in *Cross Currents* (Summer 1995), pp. 64–74.

wrong, good versus evil, duty versus privilege, and so on. "Just war theory," for example, got a new lease on life during the Gulf War crisis in 1991, with many persons insisting that there are criteria for distinguishing between just and unjust wars—criteria that are available to all rational persons, without benefit of Christian revelation. A child might state some of them thus: "It's not fair if big nations attack little nations; it's not fair to fight if you can settle things without fighting; it's not fair to hurt people more than you have to in order to win."

But there is a problem with this approach, highlighted in an ongoing theological discussion about nature versus grace, reason versus revelation, sin versus perfection—a place where Protestant and Catholic scales do tip in different directions. Reinhold Niebuhr, for example, feels that when we attempt to defend our human conduct too fully by an appeal to reason, we overlook the fact that there is no vantage point of pure disinterestedness from which we can make such judgments; our own needs and desires will influence our conclusions. We can never make an absolutely unbiased adjudication of conflicting claims, when we are among the parties to the dispute. With identical criteria for judging the Gulf War, for example, those contemporary theologians Saddam Hussein and George Bush came to identical (and therefore conflicting) conclusions: my side is completely right and just, the other is completely wrong and unjust. And we knew ahead of time where, say, members of the militant American Legion and the pacifist Fellowship of Reconcilation would emerge when they applied their "just war" criteria to the situation in the Gulf.

So let us heed the Niebuhrian warning that we will always bring *to* an issue of justice or injustice much accumulated baggage, and often prejudicial baggage, not all of which we can check at the curbside before making a decision.

For this and other reasons, I am attracted to the approach of Karen Lebacqz, professor of ethics at the Pacific School of Religion, in her book *Justice in an Unjust World*. She argues that while we have great difficulty recognizing justice abstractly, we have little difficulty recognizing *in*justice in its specificity. In doing battle against injustice, and seeking to remove it from the scene, we come to understand better the nature of what we hope to put in its place. We listen to oppressed people—victims of dictatorship, victims of torture, recipients of sex discrimination, people denied work through no fault of their own, victims of rape, gays in the military, or whatever—and by standing with them in their need we fulfill liberation theologian Juan Luis Segundo's bottom-line definition of the liberation struggle, that "the world should not be the way it is."

The Contribution of Scripture

Where, then, do we go from such a broad starting point? As a Protestant, I find a significant resource: in scripture, a position happily and increasingly shared by Catholics as well, as an examination of the 1986 Roman Catholic Bishops' Pastoral Letter on "Economic Justice for All" will corroborate.

This move to scripture is an important shift in the argument, and we should take note of that. To appeal to part of the Christian revelation is to run the risk of separating ourselves from many of those with whom we need to be in solidarity, but who have different views of scripture than we do. And I do not want to be separated from dedicated "secularists" whose devotion to the cause of justice often puts mine to shame, people who live a version of the gospel they do not consciously acknowledge. If the resources they have are ample enough to keep them going, we must say more power to them. But we have the right and even the duty to clarify for ourselves the ethos within which we as Christians seek to operate. Scripture provides at least half a dozen resources for dealing with issues of justice. And these deserve comment:

1. A creative biblical starting point is the notion of *a preferential option for the poor*. This was explicit in the deliberations of the second Vatican Council (1962–1965), as well as in various documents of Latin American bishops, and is also a common thread in recent papal "social encyclicals." It is strongly represented in the various writings of such renowned Protestant theologians as Reinhold Niebuhr and Karl Barth.

These various sources provide us with a quintessential summary of the biblical perspective: The God who loves all God's children is the God who also has a special concern for the poor. As a result, those who count themselves

a protestant view of justice

God's children have a special obligation themselves to engage in a similar preferential option for the poor. Karl Barth is unequivocal on this point:

> The human righteousness required by God and established in obedience—the righteousness which according to Amos 5:24 should pour down as a mighty stream—has necessarily the character of a vindication of the poor in favor of the threatened innocent, the oppressed poor, widows, orphans and aliens. For this reason, in the relations and events in the life of God's people, God always takes a stand unconditionally and passionately on this side and on this side alone; against the lofty and on behalf of the lowly; against those who already enjoy rights and privilege, and on behalf of those who are denied and deprived of it. *Church Dogmatics,* II:1, p. 386

As Barth reminds us, there are many admonitions in scripture to care for "the widows and orphans," a phrase that slides off our backs because of its constant repetition. We need to remember that in Israelite society, the most deprived persons were those same widows and orphans, so the rest of society was called to look after them, before any others. Today, the phrase must include all the victims of oppression—whether that oppression is personal, social, political, corporate, or even ecclesiological.

2. The preferential option for the poor is complemented with the biblical claim that *to know God is to do justice,* powerfully dramatized in Jeremiah 22:17–21. The prophet is excoriating the king—a favorite pastime of prophets—for building a palace he does not need, using the most expensive materials available, painting it in garish colors, and using slave laborers who are coerced into working for free—a classic instance of injustice. And the prophet compares the king to his father, of whom he says:

> Your father ate and drank like you,
> But he practiced justice and right;
> This is good.
> He defended the cause of the poor and needy;
> This is good.
> "Is this not what it means to know me?"
> says the Lord. (Jeremiah 22:15–16)[1]

55

The grammatical construction demands an affirmative response. This *is* what it means to know God: to do justice and righteousness, to uphold the cause of the poor and needy. To claim to know God while doing injustice is a contradiction in terms. To know God is to do justice.

To the biblical writers, God and justice are inseparable. The famous summary in Micah 6:8 (which also rolls off our backs because it is so familiar) underlines the interconnection: "What does God require of you, but to do justly, to love tenderly, and to walk humbly with God." This is not a three-step program; it is a single inclusive demand: three different ways of saying one single thing. To be doing any one of these things fully is to be doing the other two as well. We walk humbly with God by doing justice and loving mercy.

3. This emphasis on justice suggests a third strand in the biblical message, *the interconnection of justice and love*. Reinhold Niebuhr suggests a distinction between them that goes something like this: the uncalculating, selfless love of God (*agape*) is the final law of life, the ethic of the kingdom of God. But the world we live in is not the kingdom of God. So how do we approximate *agape?* We do so by engaging in the struggle for justice in a fallen world, where no choices are as pure as we would like, and no achievements are as complete as we would like. Justice seeks these approximations by engaging in necessary and inevitable compromises that we hope will move us closer to, rather than farther away from, the purity of *agape*. Niebuhr calls this task "an impossible possibility,"[2] meaning that we must continually strive for it, even though we will never fully reach it. Love without justice is naive and sentimental, but justice without love is harsh and unfeeling.

So the struggle for justice is a worthy struggle for proximate goals—this piece of legislation rather than that one, winning the strike rather than losing it, moving toward more rather than less community. *Agape* is always relevant in this struggle, for it reminds us that no matter how much we achieve in the realm of justice, we have still not reached the fullness of *agape,* and must continue our moral striving, for the kingdom of God will not have arrived when the legislation has been passed or the strike has been won.

a protestant view of justice

We frequently agree about the centrality of both justice and love, and yet disagree on next steps. We may, for example, agree on the sanctity of all life, and yet disagree on what this means in relation to birth control or abortion. We may agree that all people are made in God's image, and yet disagree on what this means in relation to people made in God's image who happen to be gays and lesbians, or about the appropriate roles for women to play in the governance of the church.

The way beyond this impasse, I believe, goes back to my first point: we must give special weight to the voices of those who are victimized; women who suffer from the fact that it is usually men who make the legislative decisions about whether a pregnancy may be terminated or not; or women who feel demeaned by church decisions about their leadership roles that are made by almost exclusively male-dominated hierarchies.

We can profit from the example of Roman Catholic Archbishop Rembert Weakland of Milwaukee, who listens not only to what male canon lawyers say about potential new roles for women in the church, but also to women leaders themselves—a new idea in Catholic thought, whose time has come, and for which the archbishop has bravely endured many rebuffs from official and unofficial sources.

4. Another part of the biblical understanding of justice is the emphasis on what we now call *social ethics,* brought to the fore by the 1966 World Council of Churches conference in Geneva on "The Church and the Social Revolutions of our Time," and the seminal Latin American Bishops' conference at Medellin in 1968, both of which gave attention to what they called "structural injustice."

When we confront injustice in the world we misunderstand it if we see it only in individualistic terms and assume that if we can just get rid of a few unjust individuals we will have cleared the path for justice. This is the great Protestant naïveté. Boards of great corporations do not ask, "How can we increase profits in such a way that children will starve?" Board members are not individual schemers against children. But it is the job of boards of large corporations to ask, "How can we increase profits, since we have a fiduciary responsibility to our shareholders?" And with the best will in the world, they may decide, let us say, to transform vast agricultural

57

acreage that sustains thousands of people into a coffee plantation as a cash crop, with the undesired side effect that children of the region *do* starve, since nutritious food is no longer grown, and no one has yet found a way to make coffee beans a nutritious diet for children.

We are not dealing here with evil individuals as much as with an entire structure, within which individuals are forced to operate, and in which, despite their individual good will, a policy may be adopted that is destructive to indigenous peoples and must therefore be opposed. Some reflection on the biblical image of "principalities and powers" of evil should be instructive at this point.

5. We must apply concerns about justice not only to others but to ourselves—*equally, and even more insistently.* The necessity for such self-criticism is writ large in the biblical tradition. It is instructive that the most searing critiques of Israel and Israelite culture come not from the Assyrians or the Babylonians or the Greeks, but from within Israel itself—from the prophets, who hold their nation to even higher standards of justice than they do the pagan nations. If our message is to have any credibility today it must consist not only of words—pronouncements of undoubted depth— but also of deeds, in the embodiment of structures of justice within our own institutional lives.

It is one of the special strengths of the previously noted U.S. Bishops "Letter on the Economy" that after a sweeping survey of our whole society and the need for more justice, it subjects the church itself to the same stern analysis and set of demands.

6. A final and difficult biblical theme is *the relationship between justice and forgiveness.* Forgiveness is the ultimate outreach of love—a willingness to be so committed to the other that one will endure whatever rebuffs the other visits upon one without retaliating in kind. Jesus' words on the cross, "Forgive them, for they know not what they do," echoed in Stephen's words while being stoned, "Do not hold this against them," and repeated through the centuries by the martyrs of the church, represent the highest expressions of *agape.* Most of us are not made of such stern stuff, and will spend our lives in an ethical twilight zone, where there are few pure choices, grubbing around in the world of proximate goals and com-

promises for the sake of getting something rather than nothing, perhaps occasionally taking our lumps for trying to be on the side of the powerless. Our lives will not be measured by our attainments — or if they are, those lives will fall far short of what love asks of us.

And so the final assurance of the gospel is that the measuring rod is not how much *we* have done, but how much *God* does for us in spite of how little we have done in return. To a person of sensitive conscience, a world without this resource of divine forgiveness would be a sheer hell of self-condemnation: how little we did compared to what was needed . . . how only in retrospect did we see issues crying for attention that we ignored . . . how destructive were some of our attempts to be constructive. . . . We know such litanies by heart, and can only be grateful that the mercy of God is more powerful than our attempts at self-justification and self-depreciation.

The good news is that such judgments are not finally in our hands. We are to work, measuring what we do not by the factor of our success but only by the factor of God's faithfulness to us. At the end of our days, the decisive matter will not be that we succeeded, but that we tried. And until that time, we are invited to share in God's concern for creating a more just world, and to recognize, beyond all slogans and theological constructions, that our bottom line is a recognition that "to know God is to do justice," and that "the mercies of God are fresh every morning."

NOTES

1. Miranda, José P., *Marx and the Bible* (Maryknoll, N.Y.: Orbis Books, 1974), 44.

2. Niebuhr, Reinhold, An Interpretation of Christian Ethics (New York, N.Y.: Harper & Brothers, 1935).

10 Bonhoeffer's Three Strategies and Their Message for Us

I want to start with an image from Dietrich Bonhoeffer, who is still important for us many years after World War II, in which he withstood Hitler to the death. He is not only important for where he arrived as a participant in the plot on Hitler's life, but where he came from. For Bonhoeffer started where many of us start—like us, he was comfortably situated, a member of the bourgeoisie, intelligent, academically inclined, and there was nothing in his upbringing that would have led even an FBI informer to tag him as a potential resister against a legally elected government. Bonhoeffer writes, with Lutheran remnants still remaining,

> There are three possible ways in which the church can act toward the state: in the *first* place . . . it can ask the state whether its actions are legitimate and in accordance with its character as state; i.e., it can throw the state back on its responsibilities.
>
> *Secondly,* it can aid the victims of state action. The church has the unconditional obligation to the victims of any . . . society, whether they belong to the Christian community or not. The command goes, "Do good to *all* people." In both these courses of action, the church serves the free state in its own free way, and at times when laws are changed [i.e., by the Nazis] the church may in no way withdraw itself from these two tasks.
>
> The *third* possibility is not just to bandage the victims under the wheel, but to put a spoke in the wheel itself. Such action would be direct political action, and is only possible and

Selections from *Moving Toward Shalom: Essays in Memory of John T. Conner,* published by the Fellowship of Reconciliation, in Nyack, New York, 1986, pp. 5–18.

desirable when the church sees the state failing its function of creating law and order, i.e., when it sees the state unrestrainedly bring about too much or too little law and order. . . . There would be too little if any group of subjects were deprived of their rights, too much law where the state intervened in the character of the church and its proclamation.[1]

All of us in the church make choices that fall somewhere along that spectrum, and most of us were forced by events in the 1960s to give serious consideration to the third response. I have only recently realized that we can occupy these positions *simultaneously as well as sequentially.*

Sequentially, we all begin at Bonhoeffer's point one: as citizens, we ask the state *to be a true state,* in our case, to fulfill its obligation of "liberty and justice for all." We try, in Bonhoeffer's phrase, "to throw the state back upon its responsibilities" by writing letters to Congress and the White House, supporting some political candidates, opposing others, and lobbying for certain kinds of legislation. The assumption is that government of, by, and for the people is responsive to the people. Blacks are slaves? We work to make that legally impossible. Women don't have the vote? We work to get them the vote. Presidents should serve no more than two terms? We pass an amendment to limit their time in office.

But calling the state to be a true state is not always a success story. The heads of state may have a different agenda, and it may embody injustice, racism, and dissimulation, so that people get hurt. We point out that we are bound by international law not to mine the harbors of another sovereign state—and our leaders scoff. We quote from the United Nations charter about the illegality of invading another country—and they pay no attention. We point out that mandatory testing for drug use makes the innocent prove that they are not guilty, rather than the other way around—and are virtually linked with the Mafia for so saying. A point comes, in other words, when we realize that no matter how loudly we speak, nobody in congress or the White House is hearing.

And while our leaders are refusing to hear, ordinary people out there are hurting. Do we wait for a perfect world before going to their aid? Of course not. And so we engage in the second tactic Bonhoeffer describes:

we "*aid the victims* of state action." We respond to the biblical injunction, "Do good to *all* people," whether Christian or not. And so we have to run soup kitchens, and provide day-care centers, and offer legal-aid services to the victims. This second position Bonhoeffer likens to following a mad driver who is careening down the main street of Berlin, running down pedestrians and leaving a bloody trail in the street. And then church folk come along in an ambulance, pick up the wounded, and try to get them to a hospital in time. It all has to be done, of course. But *it is not enough*. It doesn't get to the heart of the problem, which is the mad driver's utter disregard for anybody but himself, and our realization that he will injure still more people if he is allowed to continue driving.

So Bonhoeffer goes on, "the *third* possibility is not just to bandage the victims under the wheel, but *to put a spoke in the wheel itself*." We stop the car from careening down the street; we impede its further motion; we arrest the driver; we make sure that the car will be used carefully rather than recklessly. We say, "No more of this. You can't use the car for this purpose. We'll get another driver and put a speed regulator on the motor." This is an *act of resistance*. It is the point to which some of us are being driven by the inadequacy of the first two tactics.

But before concentrating on this third strategy, I return to my initial surprise: the discovery that all three strategies can be carried on *simultaneously as well as sequentially*. For example, not only trying to cooperate with the National Immigration Service in relation to the Refugee Act of 1980 but calling for its just application in Central America; not only helping refugees in their immediate difficulty in getting enough food, shelter, and legal aid, and not only defying the government's attempt to send refugees back to their death but establishing alternative lifelines. The strategies have been carried out simultaneously as well. If you are hiding a refugee, you are simultaneously trying to get new legislation that will make it safe for the refugee to go public, while a public act of defiance of the Immigration Service may be coupled with appeals to that same body to humanize and regularize its procedures.

In other words, to move to Bonhoeffer's third strategy does not mean turning our backs on the other two strategies. Even if we move to specific acts of resistance, we are still concerned to elect better rather than worse people to public office. Even as we bind the wounds of the victims, we are still concerned to raise the awareness of the body politic so that in the future there will be fewer wounds to bind. To move to acts of resistance does not mean to close the door to voting and lobbying, or to lose concern for remedial social services. A commitment to continue the struggle on all three fronts still remains. To put it graphically: to have opted for resistance does not mean remaining indifferent to the possibility that Pat Robertson or Pat Buchanan might someday be elected president.

The question that plagues us is, *Is this the right time?* Are things really so serious that attempts at persuasion and remedial help are insufficient? The question is not just strategic (Will resistance work?) but also moral (Is resistance responsible?). We have it on high authority that we are not to build towers or wage war without counting the cost. It might be "responsible" to take a stand even if it were not clear that it would "work," that is, we might simply be called upon by the gospel to make our witness and pay the cost. But we have to be careful not to create a situation where *other people* who trust us end up paying the cost. There is an important eleventh commandment at work here: "Thou shalt not decide that somebody else should become a martyr."

The German experience is instructive in this regard. The Barmen Declaration of the Confessing Church in Germany is part of our heritage, and we can draw strength from it fifty years after its creation. Indeed, the primary way I have heard the question of resistance focused goes, "Is it time for another Barmen?" Is it time for us to offer an unequivocal no to certain acts of our government?

The greatness of Barmen is that a tiny segment of the German church *did* speak. The tragedy of Barmen is that the speech was *too late* to be effective. Hitler's power was already so strong that neither Barmen nor the Confessing Church could stop him. The route beyond Barmen was martyrdom, and while that is a noble way to die, and may speak volumes to subsequent generations, it is not very effective in the short run. And so our question becomes, If even Barmen was too late, and we are in a situation where similar sinister scenarios are emerging, can we speak and act before it is too late for us as well?

The way to raise this question for ourselves is to ask whether or not we are at a time of what historically is called a *status confessionis,* a "confessional situation." This rather technical but crucially important term refers to a situation in which a portion of the church finally says, "We've debated the rights and wrongs of the issue long enough. Either the policy we are discussing can be supported by Christians, or it cannot. There is no longer any middle ground. It's either/or."

The Germans in the Confessing Church came to that conclusion, and "We cannot serve God and Hitler" would be a sufficient summary of Barmen's main theme. South African Christians likewise came to a similar decision about apartheid. "If you support apartheid," they decided, "you exclude yourself from the Christian fellowship."

To come to such a conclusion is serious business. Churches rarely define a situation as a *status confessionis,* and that is a good thing, for the danger of a premature *status confessionis* is that some partial truth, popular at the moment, will be elevated to the place of an eternal truth, and we will equate a particular political or social hobby horse of our own with the unambiguous will of God. But granting the dangers in moving too quickly into announcements of a *status confessionis,* the dangers of failing to take a stand are even worse. For they consign the church to timidity and caution and prudence in the worst meaning of those three terms. Karl Barth said a good word here: "Better something doubtful or overbold, and therefore in need of forgiveness, than nothing at all." We can count on enough church people to be wary of any *status confessionis* so that nothing too rash will emerge.

In this whole discussion, there is an important distinction to be made between *revolution and resistance,* as a study by the Presbyterian Advisory Council on Church and Society made clear, thereby helping to redeem ecclesial timidity. A call to *revolution,* the report stated, is based on the assumption that "the political order as a whole is illegitimate and must be totally overthrown. Nothing is deemed salvageable. This, of course, is as American as apple pie, and is the origin of our national history.

A call to *resistance,* on the other hand, is based on the assumption, as the report puts it, that "the civil order is morally legitimate but that some aspects of *our* order are demonic" (italics added). The task, then, is to call attention to the demonic policies that are gradually corrupting the life of the state, and seek to transform them before rottenness gets to the core and nothing redeemable is left. A recent World Council study, "Resistance as a form of Christian Witness," offers further help. "Resistance is an attitude of vigilance in defense of the fullness of life. It is every attitude and action, individual and corporate, which goes against powers that threaten people and God's creative work in the world." The study gives as examples of such threatening activity "economic exploitation and the marginalization or victimization of people."

Resistance, in other words, is a strategy between *reform* (which calls for small improvements but at no point significantly challenges the system as a whole) and *revolution* (which challenges the whole—hook, line, and sinker).

I do not believe we are at the point of calling for revolution, though, as I have already noted, that heritage is central to our nation's past, and we could perhaps learn to live comfortably with it. But this is *not* Hitler's Germany, though if we remain asleep it could become such. To ensure that it will not become such means resisting at those specific points where corruption is already present, not only to root it out at that point, but to ensure that by doing so we will forestall its further growth in the system as a whole. Resistance is *not* saying "everything must go and we must start all over again." Resistance *is* saying, "There are some key points where our society is succumbing to dangerous tendencies. We must note them and oppose them so that they do not infect all the other points as well."

All of us by various means of resistance—nonviolent challenge, civil disobedience, corporate or individual resistance on such levels as tax withholding, and so on—need to find the place where our yes to Jesus Christ becomes a no to our government. I think that we need to help one another, challenge one another, support one another, wherever we are on such a spectrum. But no matter where we are individually, let us be as one

65

corporately in realizing that the hour is late, that national policies calling for resistance are already in our midst, and that we must find new ways to respond.

NOTES

1. Bonhoeffer, Dietrich, *No Rusty Swords* (New York, N.Y.: Harper & Row, 1965), 225.

11 "Can We Have a Just and Compassionate Society?"

The root meaning of "compassion" is relatively clear: it comes from *cum-passio,* and means "to suffer with," to "suffer alongside the other," "to enter into and share the condition of another." Some dictionaries offer "pity" as a synonym, but my own feeling is that compassion is stronger than that, for it often involves *action* on behalf of the other, which is rooted in closeness, rather than in some abstract kind of concern that is manifested at a distance. In compassion, both geographic and psychic distances are overcome.

Passio by itself has been associated historically in Christian theology with the passion (i.e., the "suffering") of Christ on the cross. Johann Sebastian Bach's *Saint Matthew's Passion* is based on that part of Matthew's Gospel that describes Jesus' seizure, trial, and death.

But the word is not limited to suffering or to Christ. "Compassion" can describe any strong feeling for another person, as in sexual love, or for otherwise ordinary activity, such as a passion for the game of football. As the definitions of "passion" have multiplied, the special stress on *"com-*passion" as dealing with shared suffering, sympathy, and a desire to help, seems to have increased.

We do not, however, confront a decision for *either* justice *or* compassion. Unless *both* are interwoven in our understanding of society, that society will remain seriously deficient. To put it a

The title of this chapter was the theme of an international conference of Christians and Jews held in Warsaw, Poland, in 1994. This chapter is the major part of a lecture given at that conference (see chapter 9 for the initial portion of that lecture).

little too simply: justice without compassion tends to be harsh, even legalistic; while compassion without justice tends to be sentimental, even ineffective. Both must be present.

At this point, however, a voice of "realism" is likely to invade the discussion and suggest that we are trying to mix apples and oranges when we propose that both justice and compassion should be present in a creative society.

One can appropriately exhort a society to be "just," the argument would go, and to a certain degree justice can be realized within the life of a society or state. Indeed, without justice (harsh though it may be at times) we could hardly conceive of a society surviving very long without becoming repressive—simply in the interests of its survival.

But one cannot, the realist argument would continue, appropriately exhort a society to be "compassionate." Compassion works very well when individuals or small groups are involved, but in the rough and tumble of a fallen world, a compassionate society would be swallowed up by those without compassionate leanings. Let compassionate people try to live compassionately with one another, but let them not expect that compassion will "work" in the public arena.

The problem was clearly articulated by Reinhold Niebuhr half a century ago, in a book suggestively titled *Moral Man and Immoral Society.* Niebuhr argued that while *individuals* could be relatively "moral," and live by such criteria as compassion, love, and self-forgetfulness, such achievements were beyond the possibility of human *collectives,* whose moral vision extended only to ensuring that things did not get completely out of hand in a society not susceptible to gentleness or love.

The Niebuhrian thesis, however, while descriptively powerful, can be challenged from two directions. First (as Niebuhr himself later pointed out), the book title really should have been *Immoral Man and Terribly Immoral Society,* for, with all his realism, Niebuhr had not adequately measured the degree to which individuals would become more repressive in order to keep control of a society in which self-forgetfulness or love or compassion were deemed "unrealistic," and would themselves become increasingly corrupted in such alien surroundings.

"can we have a just and compassionate society?"

But there is a second challenge as well. While it can be argued that history offers virtually no examples of societies trying to live on the basis of compassion, there has recently emerged an example of a corporate attempt to do just that, and to temper justice with mercy to an unexpected degree. This example opens some doors of hope for the rest of us.

The instance is South Africa. Just over twenty years ago, toward the end of a four-week trip to South Africa, I was asked about my dominant impression. I replied that the thing I sensed most deeply was *fear,* present in all groups with whom I had met: Afrikaaners, English-speaking South African whites, blacks, coloreds, Indians, everybody. My interrogator, a white minister, replied, "I agree. *I'm* afraid, too." And then, addressing the black pastor on his right, he continued, to him, "I'm afraid that when you get power you will treat us the way we have treated you." I was struck by the fact that he did not say, "*if* you get power," as though that were debatable, but rather, "*when* you get power," acknowledging that it was a foregone conclusion, that would inevitably be marked by violence, bloodshed, torture, and revenge.

Who could fault the expectation twenty years ago that the inevitable scenario would produce still tighter repression of blacks by whites, the increasing use of force by both, and a point when black anger would surface uncontrollably and whites would respond in kind?

And yet, that's not the way the scenario finally played out. To be sure, there has been much violence in that twenty-year period, and many innocent people have been tortured and killed. But compared to an almost inevitable violent outcome, the transition of power from one group to the other was accomplished with relative calm, decorum, and compassion.

This means that the chapter I would have written a few years ago is not the chapter I am writing today. The earlier version, steeped in the realism of modern politics, would have warned that justice and compassion can almost never come together in politics; that the most we ever get are moments, flashes, intuitions; that in an ideal world justice and compassion might dwell together, but that we should never be so naive as to assume that it could happen in the "real" world, and in South Africa of all places.

Granted that the road ahead for South Africa will be long and strewn with obstacles, and that the delicate equilibrium at the time of the voting will be under constant threat. We have nevertheless seen in the case of South Africa something rarely seen in human history—the voluntary surrender of power by one group to another group, and the acceptance of power by the oppressed group without the revenge and the horror that most of the history of the human race would have led us to anticipate. Words like "reconciliation," "forgiveness," and "compassion" were on black lips and exemplified in black lives, and in a powerful symbol of new beginnings, Nelson Mandela, freed after twenty-seven years of imprisonment, instead of turning on his jailers and crushing them, invited three of them to be his guests at the presidential inauguration.

The lesson of South Africa is that *we are never entitled to close the door marked hope* and are no longer allowed to dismiss the possibility that in other places and at other times, justice and compassion can occupy the same space at the same time.

Combining Justice and Passion

How can this be? What could we learn from this recent historical example that might speak to our own diverse situations as *we* seek to combine justice and compassion? There is not space to develop a full answer to that question, but here are a few ingredients out of which we might forge some answers for ourselves:

1. There must be a *vision,* nourished by at least a few who can communicate its worth to others and build a movement committed to the long haul. Sometimes the vision is of the kingdom of God, and sometimes of a humanly constructed utopia—a distinction to which we will return.

2. At some point, *a charismatic figure* must emerge, either the originator of the vision or one who has been powerfully grasped by it early on and can win a measure of personal allegiance. His name may be Nelson Mandela (a man of compassion), or F. W. DeKlerk (a man of justice), breaking with his whole upbringing, education, and religious belief, "a traitor to his class"—both of them committed, from very different starting points, to the realization of the vision.

3. There must be a *people,* nourished by the vision and the charismatic leaders, who retain commitment for the long haul themselves–years, even decades, putting others above self and refusing to let the vision go sour.

There must be *critique from within* as well as *critique from outside.* The movement must allow—nay, solicit—critique at every point along the way. No movement can ever be so pure that it does not need this. Indeed, the movement that looks suspiciously at an inner critique will by that very fact have forfeited playing a creative role in the future. (This is especially important for those who work through religious structures, since they seem to be the most resistant of all to critique and change.)

5. Finally, the vision must have a *sustainable content.* We assume that if justice and compassion are present, a new society can emerge that will be creative for the human spirit rather than destructive. I accept the proposition and offer now a few further comments about achieving that combination, through the possible interrelationship of the symbol of the kingdom of God and the symbol of utopia.

Symbols:
The Kingdom of God and utopia

There has been a long, and, I think, unnecessary controversy among Christians over the relationship between the creation of the kingdom of God and the creation of human utopias. The conventional dispute goes something like this:

On the one hand, the creation of the *kingdom of God* is not a human construction at all. It is totally the work of God, and its even partial presence in our midst is not the result of doing good works, but is purely a gift of God, undeserved and unattainable through the exertion of human power. (Jesus' declaration in Mark 1:15 that the kingdom of God has "broken into" our world, was a call to repentance rather than a congratulatory cablegram.)

On the other hand, the proposal of a *human utopia* rests on a human rather than a divine construction. To whatever degree it is realizable, it depends on the expenditure of prodigious amounts of human effort. The sustainability of a human utopia is similarly based on human effort directed toward giving ongoing validity to the original vision.

71

Religion and Politics, Religion as Politics

All too frequently, these two visions have been seen as being in conflict with each other. The proposal to "build the kingdom of God" is seen as an act of hubris that is doomed to failure since it rejects the divine creativity and tries to substitute a human agenda in its place. Similarly, the proposal to create a human utopia is seen as a denial of the divine creativity, and becomes an instance of human beings trying to play the role of God. The posture does not measure seriously enough the power of human sin, and is doomed to failure. It assumes that there is no divine power on which to draw, and that if there is, one can give up the human struggle and simply wait for God to give the gift of the kingdom.

The two proposals thus seem to cancel each other out. To opt for the kingdom leads to human passivity, whereas to opt for the utopia is to set goals that humans are incapable of achieving. And to combine them does not seem possible, since they have such different premises.

One of the achievements of liberation theologians like Gustavo Gutiérrez has been to help us out of this quandary, and provide a frame of reference in which human striving and divine action can be related to each other. Gutiérrez talks, for example, about the human task as one of "preparing the way"— preparing the way, ultimately, for God to establish the divine kingdom in all of its fullness. Gutiérrez is quite explicit that we do not "create" that kingdom, nor do we "bring it in." What we *are* to do is to create little foretastes, here and now, of what God wills to be the ultimate expression of human life and community under God, places where signs of the nature of the kingdom are present, at least in embryo.

These will be present where starvation has been overcome or at least diminished; where the burden of proof is on the torturer rather than the tortured; where (in that wonderful phrase from the Chilean underground, which I repeat once again) "the only privileged ones will be the children." These are not "the kingdom" in its fullness, but they are tiny *foretastes* of the kingdom, and they "prepare the way" so that at the final coming of God's kingdom there will at least be the beginnings of some congruences.

The fact that the kingdom is God's gift does not for a moment rule out human activity but rather calls for it in greater measure than ever before. Indeed, those who affirm the symbol of the kingdom of God, and those who affirm the symbol of a humanly constructed utopia, can in fact join forces, each being committed, for different reasons, to a future where justice and compassion are realized together. It is a terrible waste of human energy when adherents of these two camps try to ignore, or undermine, each other.

Thus to say that we have no responsibility for "preparing the way" is the height of moral irresponsibility. There is no discrepancy between working for a better society and acknowledging, as we do so, that the final achievement of that society will not be our work but God's. Jews have the strong and stern reminders of the prophets that the transcendent God demands that humans exert themselves precisely in the direction of justice and compassion, for as we have already heard Micah declare, "What does the Lord require of you but to do *justice,* to love mercy (or *compassion*) and thus to walk humbly with God?" Christians, in addition to claiming the prophetic tradition as their own, have also from the lips of Jesus the reminder that the very mandate of the gospel, and the character of the kingdom, is that we are to feed the hungry, clothe the naked, visit the sick and imprisoned, and in other such ways continue always "preparing the way" for what will finally be not their construction but God's gift.

Happily, this is a venture in which Jews and Christians can work together, and, indeed, *must* work together, both to "prepare the way" and to welcome God's gift. As Martin Buber made clear, Jews and Christians share a messianic faith; they disagree only about the timetable for messianic fulfillment. Metaphorically, Christians anticipate a second coming while Jews still anticipate a first.

Perhaps that is all to the good, for every time Christians proclaim a little too glibly that redemption has already come in Jesus Christ, they need to be reminded by Jews and others that the redeemed world does not look very redeemed to non-Christians. Elie Wiesel has encapsulated the difference here in the faith each proclaims and the cry each retains. The Jew cries out, "The world is so evil, why does the Messiah not come?" and the Christian wonders, "The Messiah has come, why is the world so evil?" We both have a problem and we need to help each other.

The kingdom of God and human utopias are truly interwoven, and yet distinct. As long as we do not claim too much for our results, we can work and wait, without despairing, and even with hope, for God to do something with our efforts that may surpass our wildest dreams.

Resources for Hope

Where, finally, is hope to be found? No reading of the times in which we live offers much evidence for the reality of hope. And yet somehow Christianity and Judaism, religions firmly rooted in the stuff of messy human history, provide us with the resources for hope. In the shadow of Treblinka, Jews have more reasons *not* to hope than practitioners of other faiths. And yet, they *do* hope. It is not within my competence to explain that, but it is my responsibility to record it and look at it.

Elie Wiesel, commenting on Camus, says, "When there are no reasons to hope, we must invent them." Elsewhere he describes a Jewish festival in Moscow, where the rabbi forced Jews out of the synagogue and onto the streets to dance, with the admonition, "I command you to rejoice."

Even in the midst of despair, there are sometimes recollections of times when despair was not the only alternative. The text of Psalm 42–43 is a model here. Repeatedly there is an alternation between despair and hope. "Why are you cast down, O my soul, and why are you disquieted within me?" Life is the pits. And then, immediately, come the words, "Hope in God, for I shall yet praise him, my health and my salvation." Three times within the psalm the struggle between despair and hope is waged, and hope tilts the balance.

My own greatest help comes from Augustine—not from his philosophical struggles with neo-Platonism or privative evil, but from a reflective comment whose location in the Augustinian corpus I wish I could pinpoint. Augustine writes, "Hope has two beautiful daughters. Their names are anger and courage; anger at the way things are, and courage to see that they do not remain the way they are."

That is the place where we are called upon to join forces with God. Anger and courage make it possible to hope.

But there is at least one further reality that must enter a discussion such as this: a recognition that Christians (and, I believe, Jews) hold in common:

to proclaim hope—which is an undeniable part of our history as believers—is to make an eschatological statement, or, better still, *to live eschatologically.*

On the plane of history alone there will never be sufficient reason to hope. Too much evil has taken place. One cannot visit Treblinka without the appalling recognition that those who died there were forever cheated of what life on earth was meant to be for them—dare we say, of what God meant their lives to be? On the plane of history alone that wrong can never be set right. It will always be an evil fact, and anyone who fits it into a tidy scheme has betrayed the dead.

In the face of that, there *are* eschatologies that are too tidy, too neat, that restitch the fabric of history too beautifully. But, as long as we are aware of such danger, surely it is our responsibility to proclaim more than theological warnings. We must proclaim *eschatological promises.* In ways we cannot define or delimit, there can be hope lived out after such words as "nevertheless . . ." or "and yet, and yet . . ." or "despite all . . ." We cling to the promise that God is God, not a defeated angel, that nothing can finally defeat God, that God is in the midst of us when we endure evil, not elsewhere, and that in that confidence we can refuse to succumb to despair and live in hope.

Part 3.
Living and Dying and Preaching in Times of Crisis

What do we have here? We have examples of "speaking of Christianity" in relation to two martyrs, two wars, and some feisty women opening new doors toward the future.

Surely martyrdom is no longer part of our world and our belief. Wrong. Both these martyrdoms are "contemporary," meaning that they took place during our lifetimes and have meaning for us. Disseminating the facts of the martyrs' lives and the causes of their deaths is more than enough reason for including their stories here.

The women's story also tells itself. The least one can say is that those who participated in the women's story will never be the same again. Nor will the critics who could not contain their dismay and even their fear in the face of possible challenges. Score one for the future.

I include the two sermons (1) because almost twenty years passed between the occasions of their being preached, and it seems worth recording that we church folk had not acquitted ourselves with much distinction in the interval (else why two wars so close together?), and (2) because the two texts presented here, just as they were delivered, give some sense at least of how close to the extremities we were living, in which anything, including nuclear war, could have come.

12 Archbishop Romero
The Resources of an "Ordinary" Man

March 24 is the anniversary of the murder of Archbishop Oscar Romero in El Salvador. It is fitting that we reflect on the date and the death.

How *appropriate* that when his death came, he was celebrating mass, the most important thing he was ever called upon to do. This means that his life must always be seen within the context of his death, and not vice versa.

How *typical* that the mass was a memorial mass for the mother of a friend, celebrated in a small chapel, rather than a high mass celebrated in the cathedral before a congregation of thousands.

How *priestly* that the drama of Christ's shed blood, offered for the salvation of many, should be co-mingled with Oscar Romero's shed blood—a fitting sacrifice made by both, such that on this occasion the blood of one could not be distinguished from the blood of the other.

How *prophetic* that a rifle, the instrument of death in the hands of a death dealer, should be less powerful than bread and wine, the instruments of life in the hands of a life-giver, who said only days before his death that if he died, he would rise again in the hearts of the Salvadoran people—a claim for which there is ample evidence. The victory of the assassin was only a provisional victory that will finally be canceled by the power of God, wherever the story of Oscar Romero is told.

Most of us are not the stuff out of which martyrs are made, so let us not too easily put ourselves in Romero's company. Rather

Portions of a talk given at University of Notre Dame in 1994 on the fourteenth anniversary of Archbishop Romero's death.

than seeking rapport with him, let us measure the distance between himself and us. Listen to words by Romero that Jon Sobrino reports "sent chills up peoples' spines when they were pronounced, and send chills up their spines today."

> I rejoice, bothers and sisters, that our church is persecuted precisely for its preferential option for the poor. . . . How sad it would be, in a country where such horrible murders are being committed, if there were no priests among the victims. A murdered priest is a testimonial of a church incarnate in the problems of the people. . . . It is the glory of our church to have mixed its blood—the blood of its priests, catechists, and communities—with the massacres of the people, and ever to have borne the mark of persecutions. A church that suffers no persecution, but enjoys the privileges and support of the powers of this world—that church has reason to be afraid! But that church is not the true church of Jesus Christ.[1]

It makes sense to *us* to be removed from suffering, and here is Romero telling us to rejoice, not in spite of, but precisely *because* of, suffering and persecution.

Let us confront a new source for understanding Romero—the diary that he kept during the last two years of his life, available now in English as *A Shepherd's Diary* (Cincinnati: St. Anthony Messanger Press, 1993).

Most of us lack the staying power to keep going through 542 somewhat repetitious pages. But it is worth cultivating the staying power to do that, for the remarkable humanity and stature of the man emerge in his reflections on how to deal with the raw attacks of his fellow bishops, the strength he drew from offering mass, the pathos of funeral after funeral of priests and parishioners killed by the death squads, the instant decisions called for in times of crisis, the girding up of the loins to "speak truth to power," particularly corrupt power, the living and breathing and sleeping with the constant threat of death hanging over him. He was an "ordinary man," modest and "safe," or so the authorities thought. But the authorities were wrong. Within weeks of his consecration, he was both confident and "dangerous," for he took the side of the poor. When his friend Father Rutilio Grande was murdered for starting a farmers' cooperative, Romero had supported him and condemned the killers from whom death threats immediately began to arrive. Dangerous, indeed.

I have chosen five themes to illustrate something of what he became.

1. *On the importance of outside support; or, not being a loner.* Throughout his life, Romero was caught in a maelstrom of conflicting points of view, held by groups who were skilled in selling their positions to others. One could not enter the world of politics, church politics, or humanitarian concerns, without needing immediate support. I doubt if Romero ever thought he could go it alone, appealing solely to high-minded principles presented with moral clarity. He needed allies.

In addition to creating one's own allegiances *near at hand,* one needs help from those *far away.* Romero was a fairly large fish in a fairly small pond. But the pond became larger and more visible than he had anticipated. What happened in El Salvador in relation to human rights, unemployment, and death squads had tremendous repercussions in the rest of Central America and in the United States as well. He became the "voice of the voiceless" through Radio YSAX, and on any given Sunday morning during the last two years of his life, well over half the country was hearing his message. To those near at hand, his message was clear.

But Romero's voice was known far beyond the borders of El Salvador. His diary reflects this. More and more frequently he refers to interviews and press conferences with international journalists and television stations.

Partly on the wave of his growing international stature, 118 members of the British Parliament nominated Romero for the Nobel Peace Prize, an event that in turn gained him increasing international attention. A trip to the University at Louvain in Belgium to receive an honorary degree gave him another international platform to indicate why El Salvador deserved worldwide support.

A double set of dynamics is at work here. On the one hand, *he needed to share his message* that the people of a tiny nation were destroying one another—and that the civil war would continue as long as outside funding was provided to the military. On the other hand, Romero *needed to hear support for that message from others,* not to gather personal accolades but to be reassured of support from those whose moral compasses were like his own.

A similar reinforcement occurred when people from other countries visited El Salvador. A notable example was a visit from Cardinal Lorscheider of Brazil, who chose *not* to stay at the lavish quarters prepared for him, but with Romero. "This way," he said, "I show them I am with you."

Romero wrote in his diary, about a visit from a Belgian priest, Father Juan Meplanck:

> He shows great interest in and has great joy about the position of the church in El Salvador. He assured me that many people in Europe who had lost faith in the church are recovering it, thanks to the evangelical attitudes they see in the churches of Latin America. And he asked me always to maintain this credibility that, thank God, the Church in El Salvador is awakening.

In another example, Romero was at the Puebla conference of the Latin American bishops in 1979, an event that attracted media coverage worldwide. Romero was interviewed many times and realized that he had a unique opportunity to present El Salvador's plight and ask for outside help for the forces working for peace.

2. *On using the structures of the church to good advantage.* An important church institution, or structure, in El Salvador was the Catholic University (UCA), which had a superior faculty, mostly Jesuit, all of whom were committed to being servants of the church. Romero drew extensively on these leaders, especially Ignacio Ellacuria (the rector), Jon Sobrino, Ignacio Martin-Baró, Segundo Montes, and leaders from elsewhere within the church, all of whom not only strategized with Romero but made substantive contributions to his theological understanding.

A particular ongoing vexation was the constant "occupation of the cathedral" by left-wing groups. Romero himself frequently went to the cathedral to negotiate terms for vacating the building, and he seems to have established singular rapport with leaders of the various occupying forces. Think how quickly the police in the United States would be called in the face of a similar "occupation." What impressive serenity Romero brought to such crises that made every day unpredictable.

Romero's own faith was coterminus with that of the church, and he was faithful to the teaching of the church as enunciated by the Holy Father and preserved in scripture and tradition. He also realized, however, that the church, while truly the body of Christ, had a very human side, and that structures like the Curia, the Episcopate, the Cardinalate, and the Vatican were inhabited by mortal men who make decisions affecting the entire church, including that part of the church in El Salvador. In the best of all possible worlds, he knew, the church in El Salvador would be protected by, rather than threatened by, members of the Curia in Rome. But when four of the six Salvadoran bishops began to work diligently to destroy Romero, he, as a dutiful son of the church, made several trips to Rome to ensure that *his* side of the story was on record along with that of his opponents. He was no romantic about the use and abuse of power.

When going to see cardinals or prefects, or the pope himself, Romero prepared well, listened well, took advice from others about how best to present his case, and seems to have done his cause considerable good. The days in Rome were not without discouragement, however. Some interviews went better than others, and Vatican red tape sometimes bewildered him. But he kept scrupulous notes, both during and after interviews, so that the record would be as clear as possible.

3. *An interruption: on having the structures of the church used against one, and discovering that "a man's foes may be those of his own household."* God tests us in many ways, some of which, in retrospect, we can understand and accept. But for Romero, one particular burden seemed at the time, and seems even more in retrospect, to have been too much to have asked a human being to bear. For not only did Romero suffer hostility at the hands of those in the government, the military, the business world, and daily life, but, with the exception of Rivera y Damos, he also suffered hostility at the hands of his fellow bishops. The other four bishops opposed Romero on matters both substantive and procedural, attacking him in public and in private, circulating scurrilous rumors about him, going behind his back to send falsified accounts of his activities to Rome, refusing to work cooperatively, and doing everything in their power to achieve his removal from office. It is bad enough to be attacked by those with whom one shares few convictions; it is worse to be attacked by those one could have expected to be friends and allies.

That Rome did not finally accede to the other bishops' request to remove Romero is to the credit of the church. But the intense and unremitting anguish to which all this exposed Romero is to no one's credit, save Romero's; almost from the day of his consecration to the day of his murder he bore this cross of episcopal enmity, and did not let it destroy his life. It took an assassin's bullet to do that.

The attempts to undermine Romero were legendary: One of the bishops attacked the way Romero was administering the seminary and wrote to Rome transmitting false information. Two bishops worked behind Romero's back to institute changes in the statutes of *Caritas,* an archdiocesan publication, although such changes were illegal without the archbishop's approval. While Romero was at the Puebla conference, one of the bishops stirred up new trouble at home, accusing the Jesuits of going to Puebla to lobby for Romero's allegedly idiosyncratic position on the role of the church in domestic affairs. Such episodes are typical of dozens more. Two weeks before his death, Romero wrote:

> I fear, given the aggressiveness with which [two of the bishops] attacked me, that we have not achieved much with respect to deep feelings of unity. The Lord will judge. On my part, I want to offer up all these sacrifices, and all this unpleasantness so that the gospel may triumph and that we may all be converted to the truth and to the service of God and our people.

4. *On remaining clear about your task and refusing to let anyone else write your agenda.* The background of Romero's task was always *the massive poverty of the people,* to which so many in the church seemed blind. The task itself, he believed, always involves recommitment to the church's "preferential option for the poor," now thoroughly embedded in Catholic teaching. It does not mean an *exclusive* option for the poor, as though God hated the rich, but rather a decision to look at social, political, and economic issues and proposals first of all in terms of whether or not they benefit the poor.

In his espousal of this engagement with the poor, Romero was a teacher to the people, a pastor to the priests, a conscience to the state, a gadfly to the wealthy—and one who was available to all of the above. And while any social ethic must adapt to different circumstances, there is a central core to any ethic that does not yield to expediency or compromise. This central core was clear in Romero's teaching and living.

He walked a tightrope on the connection between the *pastoral ministry* of the church and the church's *advocacy* (or nonadvocacy) of particular social or political issues. As far as possible he advocated *flexibility,* as he demonstrated in his comments on one of the many occasions when the cathedral was "occupied":

In normal times, these occupations are profanations prohibited by law. . . . But *the situation is not normal,* and as Christ said, the sabbath is made for men, not man for the sabbath . . . and the occupation of churches . . . when all channels of expression have been cut off, is a minor evil.

There was also an underlying social analysis in his work and words:

[The nuncio from Costa Rica] has certain fears that the popular organizations may be communist [and this might infiltrate the church]. This factor, the fear of communism, affects some of his judgments. . . . I also see that among us anticommunism is many times the weapon that the economic and political powers use for their social and political injustices.

In one instance, after the resolution of a strike, Romero first gave thanks for the settlement but then went on to describe it as no more than a stop-gap victory. There must be further work, he commented, "to remove the *causes* of the crisis," since "they could provoke new conflict as long as the *root* of the problem is not resolved." This underdeveloped but crucial insight is part of Romero's whole approach: Band-Aid solutions cannot alone confront the deeper problems of poverty—unemployment, classism, racism, and violence.

Flexibility. Social analysis. But always Romero recognized that the church must *both announce and denounce,* trying "to be very fair, both to the position of the junta and that of the leftist opposition." He commented in his diary:

I spent more than an hour . . . presenting in my homily the three factors that can bring true liberation of the country: a spirit of poverty, a sense of God and our firm hope in the mystery of Christ. Only from this three-fold Christian perspective can a Christian view liberation. For that reason, this is not a political perspective but a pastoral one, which permits me to be autonomous and independent *in order to support what is good in any sector and also to announce what is evil in any sector.*

During the early fall of 1979 came signs that a coup was in the making, and Romero was involved in negotiations with various political forces. When the military finally did engineer a coup on October 15, Romero broadcast a pastoral statement the next morning.

In the address, he expressed thanks that there had been no shedding of blood, and he urged all Salvadorans to see that that remained the case. He encouraged the people to act wisely, to be patient, and to not rush to take up arms or engage in sabotage.

Romero had hard words for those who support the military coup for their own economic or political gain, charging that "They should listen to the voice of the Lord himself, who calls them to be converted." He invited those who were active in political parties and popular organizations "to show true political maturity, flexibility and a capacity for dialogue."

Finally, after telling the new government that he had studied the official declarations, he continued:

In them we can see goodwill, clarity of ideas and a clear awareness of their responsibility. Nevertheless, we want to make it very clear that this government will deserve the confidence and the cooperation of the people only when it demonstrates that the beautiful promises contained in its proclamations, issued this morning, are not merely hollow words, but a true hope that will begin a new era in our country.

5. *On cultivating the resources necessary for growth and survival.* As we have seen, Romero's was a life more than ordinarily beset with tension. How did he cope?

It is clear that for Romero there was no final division between the "outer" and "inner" life. Every day, no matter what was brewing, *he celebrated mass,* sometimes two or three times a day, and it is clear from his diary that this was of central importance to him.

Another resource was *his ongoing dialogue with the Bible.* Romero preached regularly, following the prescribed lectionary readings, relating what was happening at that moment in El Salvador to what was happening at that moment in the biblical narrative. He reported during a hectic time in national politics, a day full of violence, death, and confirmation classes and committees, that he spent the remaining time "preparing my homily and meditating on the situation in the country."

Perhaps Romero's greatest source of strength was that *he stayed close to the people.* His diary is full of accounts of going to outlying regions in rural areas, places of genuine physical danger, to say mass or hold confirmations or talk with the *campesinos.* He apparently needed this kind of physical contact as a counterbalance to the frenetic activity in the capital city, where he was continually approached by advocates of virtually every kind of political agenda. Duty alone could not have been a sufficient motivation for his outgoingness. His motivation must have been love.

As the pressures became stronger and the dangers of assassination increased, Romero could have been forgiven for muting his voice or decreasing his public activities. But he became more outspoken than ever, particularly in the homilies that reached over half the nation every Sunday. He told the soldiers not to fire their weapons. He asked President Carter to stop the flow of cash and arms to the Salvadoran military. He exposed the junta's so-called "agrarian reform" as a sham.

While others became more fearful, Romero became more outspoken. Death threats, routine during his earlier ministry, escalated. The government (which did not want a martyr on its hands) repeatedly offered him the protection of body guards. Romero refused each time, unwilling to have special treatment. In the midst of all this he could still talk about his likely death, and his hope that it could be used to further the cause of the people. He became freer in the midst of daily danger.

We refer to March 24 as the anniversary of Romero's death. But that is not sufficient identification. For when the concept of death and the concept of Romero meet, it is the concept of death that changes. We know that the impact of Romero's life is more powerful now than it was on earlier celebrations of his death. He has indeed risen again in the hearts of the Salvadoran people. He continues to do so. His commitment to the "preferential option for the poor" engages more Salvadorans than ever before. His message of hope and his disavowal of violence are a greater challenge to us than they were during his "lifetime." His future as a saint of the church is already assured, whatever official steps are or are not taken.

In Romero's diary, a man named Rebén Zamora and his wife, Doña Ester, visit Romero, and in an act of solidarity she offers to work full-time in the chancery office without pay—a clear challenge to the death squads who have already killed her husband's brother. Today we link their names with that of Romero. Rubén Zamora is a significant leader in the new El Salvador, and will remain such, whatever new political configurations emerge in subsequent years, as will also Doña Ester, working within the structure of the church itself.

The spirit of Romero is contagious and continually enlists the Zamoras and others like them. Such people make Romero our contemporary.

NOTES

1. Sobrino, Jon, *Archbishop Romero* (Maryknoll, N.Y.: Orbis Books, 1990), 38.

13 Re-Imagining Our Faith
The Resources of Some Extraordinary Women

The facts are clear. What the facts mean is still unclear.

The facts: From November 7 through November 11, 1993, almost 2200 women (and 83 men) met in Minneapolis to consider the theme of "Re-imagining God, the community, the church." The conference was sponsored by four interdenominational Minnesota church groups, with funding from mainline U.S. denominations, and attracted delegates from forty-nine states and twenty-seven foreign countries. The largest single delegation was 409 Presbyterians, closely followed by 391 United Methodists, 313 Lutherans, 234 Roman Catholics, and 144 from the United Church of Christ. In a mix of plenary sessions, workshops, liturgies, dance, poetry, and conversation tables, the participants engaged in "re-imagining" many theological claims, both domestic and international. As one description put it: "Provocative presentations were made by speakers representing a variety of theological viewpoints. Participants were challenged to think about and discuss, but not necessarily agree with, the views expressed."

So much for the facts. What do they mean?

That depends on who is talking. For most of the delegates the conference was a moving, empowering, stretching experience, as hundreds of evaluations by attendees make clear. For a few other attendees (and especially for several reporters covering the conference for *The Presbyterian Layman*) the conference was "blasphemous," characterized in the *Layman* as an effort "to recreate

God." The activities of the conferees were described as "destroying traditional Christian faith, adopting ancient pagan beliefs, rejecting Jesus' divinity and his atonement on the cross, creating a god(dess) in their own image, and affirming lesbian lovemaking."

An unofficial newspaper, published by conservative Presbyterians, with a well-deserved reputation for distortion of fact and stridency of tone, led the attack. Without its demands for Presbyterian staff firings, heresy trials, or their equivalent, and a proposal to withhold congregational funds in protest, thus crippling the access to ongoing fundings, the impact of the conference would probably have been less sensational to the world outside and still deeply empowering to the delegates inside. As the chairman of the Presbyterian Lay Committee asked rhetorically, "If our reporters had not covered this event, how long would such a trend in our church have gone unnoticed or unchallenged?"

In the best of all possible worlds, one could ignore such reporting. But in a fallen world, institutions and individuals must defend themselves if only to set the record straight. The tragedy is that as such conservative journals in all denominations increase their pressures for staff firings and withholding funds, the ensuing discussion will only become a more acrimonious and destructive exercise in bloodletting. Genuine theological issues that deserve discussion will continue to be lost in a journalistic smoke screen. I propose, therefore, to try to disengage from heated discussion and initiate a theological defense of the conference that I hope will raise the level of exchange.

1. The appropriateness of the conference is beyond challenge and must be supported. The great theological hallmark of the church, at least since the sixteenth century, has been *Ecclesia reformata sed semper reformanda,* the church reformed but always in process of being reformed. The theological task is never completed. We must always be ready for new openings from the Spirit. Whenever proposals for new language or imagery are made, as in the case of the re-imagining conference, the project should be welcomed and its results examined *responsibly,* whether there is full agreement on the substance of the proposals or not.

I can illustrate this need by an example from the history of my own denomination, the Presbyterian Church (U.S.A.). When our General Assembly adopted a new confession in 1967, this was a clear decision by our highest judicatory that our formal doctrinal standard, the Westminster Confession of 1647, was no longer an adequate vehicle by which to communicate the faith in 1967. In an attempt to answer questions people were asking in those derisive years of the 1960s, the new confession was built structurally around the theme of *reconciliation.*

In addition, the General Assembly adopted a *group* of confessions, eight in number, from different periods in the history of the church, to drive home the point that *all* theological statements fall short of adequacy. This is true even of Presbyterian statements, and the best we can ever do when confronting infinite mystery with finite words is to touch the outer shadows of that mystery. Every attempt to rearticulate the faith for a new day deserves to be taken seriously, whatever our final assessment of the proposal may be. This is what the conference on re-imagining was all about.

2. A second theological principle, the priesthood of all believers, is a recognition that those who speak (within the church and for the church) constitute a wider body of contributors than ever before. One can now be a theologian without being ordained; one can now hold office within the church without being male (though that concept is still far from receiving universal recognition); one can now reflect, speak, write, discuss, and act while still a layperson.

The shape of the re-imagining conference was determined by the fact that virtually all the delegates, speakers, and liturgists were women. Let the record also show that not only were outstanding leaders from the United States present but delegates from overseas included a veritable who's who of theologically trained ecumenical leaders, such as Chung Hyun Kyung (Korea), Mercy Amba Oduyoye (Ghana), Ophelia Ortega (Cuba), Kwok Pui-Lan (Hong Kong), Elsa Támez (Costa Rica), and others equally qualified.

The gender makeup of the conference should be viewed as an emphatic plus rather than an implicit liability. Never before, surely, has there been a similar occasion when the viewpoints, cultural gifts, and re-imaginings of women could be stated so clearly and strongly. I hope this was a significant gift to all the women who attended. I hope even more that it may be a gift to male church members as well, who will view this conference as the beginning of a new dialogue. Instead of depending on old images, as men have done for centuries, perhaps we can hear for the first time how sensitive, committed, theologically trained women are re-imagining God and Jesus and the church, in analogies out of their own experience. Male images no longer speak as clearly to women as they once did. Women have recognized this and are now creating their own. And if such feminine images do not yet speak to men, it is time for men to listen more carefully.

3. Our *use of scripture* is a further arena for fresh thinking. It should be no threat to the authority Christians accord scripture to affirm that the Bible is in part a product of the culture(s) in which it was written, and that the events it reports are interpreted almost entirely by men. Many of the Bible's culture-bound concepts are no longer appropriate or even true — the condoning of slavery, for example, or God's rebuke to Saul for *not* killing all the men, women, and children of the Amalekites.

I see no possible way to deny this patriarchal slant in the scriptures. Critics of the conference were appalled at such challenges to Holy Scripture. But it is essential to acknowledge the truth about the origins of our documents and work together — men and women — to develop new forms of exegesis that do not perpetuate patriarchalism. As one of the delegates, Johanna Bos, put it, "We have not come here to jump on the feminist bandwagon, but to upset the patriarchal applecart." This is not only a memorable figure of speech, but a deep truth as well, and our concrete response to the conference ought to be to bring men to see the truth of our unrecognized patriarchy. (See Johanna Bos's book, *Reimagining God: The Case for Scriptural Diversity* [Louisville, Ky.: Westminster John Knox Press, 1995].)

4. In the church as a whole, and among the critics of the conference, few things are feared more than *homosexuality,* and lesbians at the conference were almost automatically attacked by the conference's critics for "celebrating" their sexual orientation. One is entitled to ask, however plaintively or angrily, what else are lesbians out of the closet supposed to do? My own denomination has hardly demonstrated courage in this matter, proffering at most a constitutionally validated welcome to membership for lesbians

and gays, but simultaneously a constitutionally validated warning that homosexual ordination is beyond the Presbyterian pale. In the course of reaching this decision, the church mandated three years of "study" of and dialogue about homosexuality, but under conditions that made it exceedingly risky for closet lesbians and gays to declare openly who they are.

Under this cloud (and the situation is similar in most other denominations), it is a sign for rejoicing that the conference *did* welcome and celebrate lesbians in attendance. There are few other places within the church where that can happen today.

5. Probably the greatest controversy engendered by critics of the conference centered on claims that Delores Williams, professor of theology and culture at Union Theological Seminary, had denied the contemporary importance of *the doctrine of the atonement*. Without putting words in her mouth (Delores Williams is quite capable of speaking for herself), let me suggest a few items that should go into our appraisal of such a charge.

We need to remember first of all that by A.D. 451 the church had arrived at a consensus on the doctrine of the *incarnation* (who Christ *is* for us) that has stood the test ever since, but that by contrast the church has never been able to arrive at a similar consensus on a doctrine of *atonement* (what Christ *does* for us). A number of attempts have been made throughout church history, but no one of them has ever been deemed adequate to contain the fullness of Christ's coming to us.

As a consequence there are more than half a dozen doctrines of the atonement, known by such key words as "ransom," "satisfaction," "substitution," "moral influence," "Christus Victor." They have partially, but never fully, captured the meaning of Christ's death on the cross as the vehicle of our redemption. This means that Professor Williams is only doing her job as a teacher in searching for newer and more adequate ways to re-imagine redemption, particularly for African-American and all third world women.

She believes that traditional atonement doctrines focus so much on Jesus' suffering and shedding of blood that they have actually been detrimental rather than helpful. She sees such doctrines being used to keep African American women subservient, telling them that they must submit to authority and be content with their lot, accept their lot meekly, endure suffering without complaint, and pass on to their children a view of life that exalts undeserved and unchallenged suffering.

If that is indeed the message our present teaching about atonement communicates to the poor of the world, then we must surely let it go and continue the church's never-ending search for new ways of understanding God's saving action. Professor Williams in fact did so with extraordinary creativity in portions of her talk not emphasized by the press. She proposed that we must see Jesus as a sign of *life* rather than death, a sign of courage and militancy in the face of what is wrong, rather than a sign of passivity, accepting a human existence God surely wants no one to endure. (She has elaborated on these themes in *Sisters in the Wilderness,* Orbis Books, 1993, esp. pp. 161–67.)

The re-imagining conference presented us with the gift of a challenge to seek new ways of talking about God's being at one with us (at-one-ment) so that we may recover "good news to the poor" and also to us.

6. There was, if possible, even more misunderstanding centered on the specific *re-imagining of God* at the conference, both liturgically and imagistically, than on the doctrine of atonement. For conference planners charged with devising a shared liturgical experience for almost 2200 women from varied liturgical and theological backgrounds, it was clear that "the sacrament of the Lord's Supper" as understood in, say, Presbyterian or Methodist terms, could hardly be imposed on Roman Catholics, Orthodox, Anglicans, and others, in ways that would unite rather than further divide. So rather than closing with a eucharist from which many people would feel excluded, the decision was made to have a ritual of milk and honey, drawn from the Hebrew scriptures, centering on an image of God described as Wisdom (*Sophia*), and also widely reported in the Christian scriptures, in the Synoptics, Pauline writings, and the Johannine literature.

Marcus J. Borg has provided extensive material about Jesus as Wisdom (*Sophia*) in chapters 4 and 5 of *Meeting Jesus Again for the First Time* (San Francisco: Harper Collins, 1994). *The Oxford Dictionary of the Christian Church,* published decades before the present controversy, magisterially proclaims, "In the NT Divine Wisdom is incarnate in Christ. . . . Many of the Greek Fathers, following the terminology of the OT and St. Paul use Wisdom as a synonym for the Incarnate Word or Logos" (*The Presbyterian Layman,* p. 1471). So much for the erroneously reported claim that the Minneapolis conference had created a goddess.

The last word has not been written on the relation of the image of Sophia to other images of God in scripture and tradition, but the importance of Sophia was signally highlighted at the conference, for here was an image of God to which women could relate, since the word is feminine, rather than being a patriarchal male image of force or power or kingship or battle leader. Nor has the last word been written on how best to present the recently discovered image of Sophia to an untutored world. The invocation of Sophia at the conference included graphic and sensuous imagery from which a number of the delegates, both liberal and conservative, wanted to distance themselves, at least in retrospect. But the exact role of Sophia is a matter for ongoing discussion, textual study, liturgical adaptation, and so on. To repeat: whatever else Sophia is, she is not the pagan goddess the critics created.

I want to conclude by shedding my reportorial role. Many staff people who planned and supported the conference instantly became targets of right-wing constituencies and were told that some bloodletting is the cost of survival, and that those who *do* survive had better be very clear that such forward-looking activities in the future will hasten their own professional demise. The new word will be "conformity"; the new motto, "Play it safe."

It would be a disaster if this were to happen, not only because it would provide a "victory" for the forces of reaction, but more importantly because it would inhibit, if not destroy, the kind of theological venturesomeness that must characterize any church that deserves to make it into the twenty-first century. Certainly there were enough new elements at the Minneapolis conference to give everybody something to question, but the many new directions sketched out will certainly be reflected on, discussed, written about, lived out, and tested, to see whether they represent signal advances in our theological understanding, or cul-de-sacs that lead us nowhere.

Living and Dying and Preaching in Times of Crisis

From this perspective, I urge readers to thank those who set the Minneapolis agenda—thank them for taking on difficult issues with courage, and proposing new images, many of which will illumine rather than obscure our ongoing theological journey, both as individuals and as church. We are indebted to the planners, and must support them in the midst of whatever future attacks and vilifications they may have to endure—this not only for their sake, but through them for the sake of the church as well.

14 Judgment and Joy

A Christmas Eve Sermon during the Bombing of Hanoi

The light shines on in the darkness, and the darkness has never quenched it.
—John 1:5

I'm sure some of you are saying to yourselves, "I hope this is one time he leaves politics out of the pulpit."

A fair enough request. This is, after all, the night of the angel's song, the shepherd's journey, the holy family at the manger. This is the night for tenderness and joy, for beautiful carols and soft candlelight.

I agree. Oh, how I agree! How much I would like to leave it that way. When we planned this service, we thought, very foolishly, that by Christmas Eve a peace treaty would be signed. I had even prepared (as you can see from the program) a story about some auto mechanics and computer specialists bearing gifts to the infant son of Joe Millstein and Mary Cohen Millstein, of Milpitis, California—a son who was born in the garage behind a motel on highway U.S. 17, because there was no room in the motel. Maybe I'll tell that story some other Christmas Eve. But not this one. For the promised peace treaty has been replaced by the ugly insanity of the most massive bombing raids in history. So you're going to hear a sermon . . .

The Christmas Story and Its Politics

First, a word about "Christmas and politics." I remind you that when I speak from a pulpit, as I do on this occasion, I am not

Preached in Stanford Memorial Church, Stanford University, Stanford, California, on Christmas Eve, 1972.

simply indulging in a few reflections that might be titled, "Bob Brown Looks at Life." No, when I speak from here, I am trying to bring the weight of the Jewish and Christian traditions, as contained in our scriptures, to bear on the events of the time in which we live. So although I would like to ignore politics tonight in dealing with the Christmas story, I cannot—for the simple reason that *the Christmas story itself is all wrapped up in the world of politics.*

How does Luke begin his version of the Christmas story? With references to two politicians: "In those days a decree went out from *Caesar Augustus* that all the world should be enrolled. This was the first enrollment when *Quirinius* was governor of Syria." And how does Matthew begin? With reference to another politician: "Now when Jesus was born in Bethlehem of Judaea in the days of *Herod* the King." Herod, indeed, figures prominently throughout the entire Matthew story. He is extremely worried that his power might be challenged, so he enters into secret negotiations with a group of wise men from the east, but he is using the bargaining table only to trick them. He will use them to get what he wants. They are warned by God to have no more to do with him, and so, after having visited Bethlehem, the three heads of state return home another way.

There is more to the story, such as Herod's insane use of power, as we will see in a moment. But for now, the point is that the Christmas story, for all its winsome beauty, is set firmly in the midst of a political situation—a situation in which the brutal power of a Herod is pitted against the apparent powerlessness of a tiny baby. We sentimentalize the story if we ignore the brutal context in which it is set, just as we would sentimentalize its retelling tonight if we ignored the brutal reality in which its retelling is set—the most massive bombing raids in history, being conducted in the name of our country. If the Christmas story made no sense back then apart from *its* political context, it can make no more sense today apart from *our* political context.

In that context, the juxtaposition of the story with the political situation tells us at least two things. The first is a word of *judgment,* and the second is a word of *joy.* We will come to the joy, before we leave tonight, but we can come to it authentically only through the route of judgment.

Judgment

So hear first the word of *judgment*. The Christmas story confronts us with an either/or, not a both/and. It confronts us with a *choice*.

To see how that choice is spelled out, follow the Matthew story a little further. After the wisemen have left, Herod is incensed that he has not been able to get his own way with them. As a result, Jesus, Mary and Joseph have to flee the country; Herod's wrath has made them refugees. Matthew tells us that Herod "was in a furious rage, and he sent and killed all the male children in Bethlehem and in all that region who were two years old or younger." Not having gotten his own way at the conference table, Herod lashes out vindictively at people who had no part in the dealings at the conference table. Not being a modern ruler with napalm or bombers at his disposal, he resorts to swords, but the intent and the result of both sets of actions are the same: death. Since he can't get the baby he wants directly, he will destroy all the other babies in the area, and maybe if he spreads the net wide enough, he might get the one he is really after. It is exactly the logic of a B-52 raid.

The story is called, in Christian history, the "slaughter of the innocents." It is an ugly tale. It has been repeated many times in human history. It is being repeated this very minute as the "slaughter of the innocents" goes on in Hanoi.

So the Christmas story confronts us with an emphatic either/or: either Christ or Herod. Spell that out any way you like: either truthfulness or deception. Either love or rage. Either the power represented by a baby's birth or the power represented by military might. Either/or. You can't have it both ways. You can't affirm the power of the manger and also the power of Herod. You can't both tell the truth and deceive. You can't combine love and blind rage. You can't say, "We really believe that the Prince of Peace is in that manger," and then argue that you are pursuing the way of peace by indiscriminately destroying not only two-year-olds but women, children, the aged, embassies, hospitals, and POWs, with a rain of terror from the skies.

So let me say it as plainly and as unambiguously as I can, more plainly and unambiguously than I have ever said it in my whole life, bringing all the weight I can bring of twenty-eight years as an ordained minister, who has devoted his professional and personal life to trying to understand the meaning of the Christian heritage: To those of you who are *Christians,* I assert categorically that from the standpoint of the Christian faith, there is no possible way to justify this insane escalation of the bombing. It is the way of Herod, not the way of Christ.

To those of you who are *Jews,* I do not bring the authority of an ordination you acknowledge, but I do bring at least the authority of a lifetime of study of the Jewish and Christian scriptures, and I assert categorically that from the standpoint of the God who commands us to do justly, and to love mercy and to walk humbly with God and humankind, there is no possible way to justify this insane escalation of the bombing. I do invoke the authority of my dear friend Rabbi Abraham Heschel, who died yesterday, and who said to me on the phone only three days ago, "The new bombing is an unspeakable outrage against human dignity."

To those of you who call yourselves neither Christians nor Jews, but who participate in a perspective in which every one of us in this chapel participates, the perspective of *a commonly shared humanity,* I assert categorically that from that perspective, likewise, there is no possible way to justify this insane escalation of the bombing.

So I say, considering well the implication of what I say, that if you approve of what our country is now doing in Vietnam you forfeit the right to call yourself a Christian or a Jew or a human being. If you call yourself a Christian or a Jew or a human being, then you must not only cry out in opposition to what our country is doing, so that your voice is heard across the land and across the world, but you must find whatever ways are in our power to demand an end to the grotesque contrast between the Christmas season and the way our nation is celebrating the Christian season. The Christmas message from the sky was "Peace on earth, goodwill to all peoples." The American message from the sky is "Death, death, and still more death." Either/or.

Either/or. If you attempt to combine these messages—the message of Christmas and the message of Herod—you are guilty of duplicity and lies, as are the leaders of our nation. Jeremiah described such people centuries ago, in words that could have been written for this past week. Listen: "Everyone deals falsely . . . saying 'Peace, peace,' when there is no peace" (Jeremiah 6:13–14). Every presidential appointee with a shred of moral integrity should resign in protest over the double-dealing of this administration.

So the Christmas story is a stern judgment on what our nation is doing — engaging in barbaric destruction, in a wanton and insane fashion, the largest nation on earth petulantly flexing its muscles and telling a tiny nation that we will have our way with it no matter how many of its people we have to destroy. Period.

Joy

We've usually chosen Herod. And even when we don't, we have to reflect that the cards are pretty well stacked in Herod's favor. After all, he's got the bombers. What power has a baby against a bomber? What chance has love against hate? What chance has truth against lies, particularly when the tellers of the lies have control of the media? What chance has compassion when power-hungry leaders appear to go berserk? It is enough to lead us to despair.

Yes, it *is* enough to lead us to despair, to the very edge of despair. But only that far. For there is still a joy in the Christmas message as well as a judgment. And the *final* word, after the word of judgment, has to be that word of *joy*. And I now affirm to you, just as categorically as I affirmed some other things a few moments ago, that if we will truly confront the judgment, we can also, this night, embrace the joy. We can sing, and mean it, "*Joy* to the world." We can say, and mean it, "*Merry* Christmas." We can sing, as the choir will presently sing for us, "Good Christian Men, *Rejoice*" and "God Rest Ye *Merry*, Gentlemen."

Why? What kind of crazy logic makes it possible, in the face of the darkness we so clearly acknowledge, to talk this way, to act this way? The answer is found in the affirmation we heard a few moments ago in the reading from John (1:5), about the meaning of the presence of love and hope and joy in a world that is so very dark — love and hope and joy being symbolized by the theme of light. What does John say? Listen: *"The light shines on in the darkness, and the darkness has never quenched it."* That is why we can go on, that is why we are not entitled to the luxury of despair or inaction, that is why we can affirm joy: because "the light shines on in the dark, and the darkness has never quenched it." Incredible? No, not "incredible," but rather the only thing worth investing with credibility in this time of darkness.

It is a time of thick darkness. I believe that it is worse now than it has ever been in the long history of this war. But, says John, there is a light in the darkness. No matter how thick the darkness, it is not all-engulfing. No matter how close it comes to destroying, it cannot destroy totally.

What is the nature of this light? The Christian sees this light focused in the Messiah who has come. That is what we have been singing about all evening. The Jew sees the light focused in the Messiah who is still to come. For both Jew and Christian, the light has been from the beginning, it is at the very foundation of all things, and for both Jew and Christian, in the end it will be all in all. For those who call themselves neither Jews nor Christians, there is still the light that is unquenchable in the human breast, the light of tenderness, hope, joy, compassion, love.

These things seem very frail, in the light of the ancient Herod's swords and the modern Herod's B-52s. But we are called upon to make the affirmation that their apparent frailty is stronger than all the B-52s, all the diplomatic deceptions, all the lies, all the broken promises, all the cries of "Peace, peace," when there is no peace. "The light shines on in the darkness, and the darkness has never quenched it." The gamble I ask you to make again tonight with me is the gamble that that is true; that the light *does* "shine on," as John says. It did not shine just once, it still shines; and "the darkness has never quenched it," nor will it ever do so. *The baby is finally more powerful than the bomber.*

That is the gamble, or to call it now by its right name, that is the faith that has sustained the Jews through millennia of darkness, through catastrophe after castastrophe. It is the light that has sustained Christians when they derided naive and foolish sentimentalists. It is the faith that can sustain all human beings who will forfeit their easy securities in naked power and B-52s, and affirm instead that the other things the Christmas story talks about—joy and hope and love—are the things that are most worthwhile and most enduring, because they are, as the choir will now remind us, "Of the Father's love begotten, ere the worlds began to be," and, *that* being so, are eminently trustable.

15 Becoming Peacemakers in Time of War

They will beat their swords into ploughshares, and their spears into pruning hooks. Nation will not take up sword against nation, neither shall they learn war any more.

Micah 4:3

Micah 4:3 is what we call an "eschatological vision," a beautiful statement of the kind of world we'd like to live in and bequeath to our children. But it doesn't correspond to the world we actually live in. And so the number-one question always becomes: How do we get from here to there, from our world to that kind of world? How can we be peacemakers in time of war?

Kurt Vonnegut, in *Slaughterhouse Five,* describes a World War II movie that Billy Pilgrim saw on late night television. Since Billy Pilgrim had a tendency to go into time warps, he saw the movie backward, as Vonnegut describes it:

American planes, full of holes and wounded men and corpses, took off backward from an airfield in England. Over France, a few German fighter planes flew at them backward, sucked bullets and shell fragments from some of the planes and crewmen. They did the same for wrecked American bombers on the ground, and those planes flew up backward to join the formation.

The formation flew backward over a German city that was in flames. The bombers opened their bomb bay doors, exerted a miraculous magnetism which shrunk the fires, gathered them into cylindrical steel containers, and lifted the containers into the bellies of the planes. . . .

A sermon preached in St. Mary's Cathedral, San Francisco, in 1991, during the military buildup for the bombing of Iraq.

becoming peacemakers in time of war

When the bombers got back to their base, the steel cylinders were taken from the racks and shipped back to the United States of America, where factories were operating night and day, dismantling the cylinders, separating the dangerous contents into minerals. . . . The minerals were then shipped to specialists in remote areas. It was their business to put them into the ground, to hide them cleverly, so they would never hurt anybody ever again.[1]

That's turning swords into ploughshares! It involves nothing less than reversing the whole history of human culture. Unfortunately, we can't do it by entering time warps. We have to work right where we are, knowing that time (for those of us not named Billy Pilgrim) goes in only one direction: forward. And right now, that forward direction has devastating implications. So how can we become peacemakers in time of war?

Our administration has an answer as old as the cavemen. The way to make peace is to wage war. Destroy the village in order to save it. Destroy human beings in order to save humanity. Cosy up to dictators if they serve our national interest. That is the way to make peace.

If a compelling case can be made for this position, it has yet to be made by the administration. The reason is that no amount of rhetoric can make a self-contradictory proposition plausible.

A second, more appropriate, way to be a peacemaker in time of war is to embody a style of life that puts peacemaking at the top of one's agenda, saying, for example, "Under no circumstances will I kill a single human being, *nor* will I stand idly by when my nation proposes to kill human beings wholesale." This is the pacifist decision. There are no advance assurances that it will "work," but there is tremendous assurance that the witness is essential, especially in time of war, as a reminder to all others that there must be a "more excellent way" than human slaughter.

A third way to be a peacemaker in time of war is to keep reminding people of the need for criteria by which to evaluate whether or not a given war can be called "just"—having such criteria helps to establish that all other means of settling the dispute must have been clearly exhausted. Roman Catholic Archbishop Quinn of San Francisco has recently reminded us that the war about to break out in the Middle East fails to meet this and other criteria of just war, and that members of the religious community cannot support it. The argument does not pertain only to Catholics; it is simply an appeal to reason and goodwill, characteristics present in abundance here tonight.

It is my educated guess that few people here tonight accept the so-called logic of the administration's position, and that most of us stand in some kind of relationship to either the pacifist or the just-war tradition, even if we do not use those precise words. Mr. Bush wants to be known as "the education president," but unless he is persuaded to change course he will, against his own wishes, go down in history as "the killer president." Let us, out of pastoral concern for him as well as for the lives of tens of thousands of innocent human beings, save him from that fate. So here are some of the things we must say and do in the days and nights ahead. You may expand the list at will. In moving in this direction we cannot escape becoming "political," because there is absolutely no way to separate religion and politics.

First, we must keep insisting that *the burden of proof is always on those who desire to wage war,* and never on those who want to avoid war. The initial presumption must always be that war is wrong, and that if there are ever any exceptions to that claim, they can be advanced only when all other options have unequivocally failed. It is manifestly *not* true, for example, that "sanctions have failed," or that "negotiations are now impossible," and that *therefore* war is legitimate. Five months of sanctions is not long enough to test that proposition, as expert after expert has tried to say to the administration. Patience on this score far outweighs the administration's apparent desire to rush headlong into war—a war that, however quick, "surgical," or otherwise, will still cost thousands, and probably tens of thousands, of human lives. We must bring sanctions and diplomacy back to center stage as honorable alternatives to carnage.

Second, we must continue to *challenge the president's continued usurping of power.* Even *Newsweek* (hardly a journal of the far left) has described Mr. Bush as the only hawk in the entire administration, and yet *he* is the one who claims the power to begin a war without approval of Congress. He tells us that he has "crossed the Rubicon" on the matter of violence. When he deployed two hundred thousand additional troops to the Middle East two days after the election, he did so unilaterally. He turned his back on the people and now tries to claim that the people are behind him. We must pressure Congress not only *not* to give him more power but to circumscribe the power he has already usurped.

Third, we must *refuse to be mesmerized by White House rhetoric*. Just one example: the latest rhetorical gambit charges that by permitting Secretary of State Baker to meet with his Iraqi counterpart Tariq Aziz, Mr. Bush has gone "the last extra mile for peace." What a travesty! Consultation between the two men should have been sought months ago as a *first* exploratory step rather than a *last* so-called "heroic" step. To say that the meeting will exhaust all alternatives to war makes a mockery of language, let alone morality.

Fourth, let us find new words and mount new actions in *repudiation of the present policy*. Mr. Bush claims that Saddam Hussein does not hear him; we must claim that Mr. Bush does not hear *us*. So let us remind him again that from our perspective the war he proposes to wage would be an incalculable obscenity, and here I refer to the root meaning of that word, meaning "disgusting, repulsive, and coarse." Let us remind him that if such a war starts and people (as the saying goes) "rally around the president," we will *not* be among those people. Let us lobby our congressional leaders not to support such a war. Let us support young men and women who declare that they will not fight in such a war and at whatever personal cost will declare themselves "conscientious objectors." (Some of them are here tonight and we assure them of our unequivocal support.) Let us work for the removal from office of those who support the war. And positively, let us support *all* efforts, in the European community or the world community, to find a formula for peace, rather than continuing to give license to our president to make war inevitable.

Perhaps all that sounds more like a political pitch than a sermon. So let me remind you, in conclusion, of the words in Micah just preceding the injunction to turn swords into ploughshares and spears into pruning hooks. Representing the very best of the Jewish prophetic tradition, Micah affirms that "God will judge between many nations, and arbiter among great and distant nations" (Micah 4:3, Revised English Bible). Micah is telling us, in other words, that we are not alone in this struggle. We are at the very place where *God* also is, and where God demands that *we* be. God arbitrates, as Micah puts it, by using *us* as instruments for the fulfillment of the divine purposes. And no matter what tradition we stand in, let Micah's words bind us more clearly to one another this night, so that we can all go forth from this place dedicated to the mother of the Prince of Peace and sharing a common conviction that nation must *not* take up sword against nation, neither must they learn war any more.

NOTES

1. Vonnegut, Kurt, *Slaughterhouse Five* (New York, N.Y.: Dell Publishing Co., 1968), 74–75.

16 The Wondrous Mystery of the Efficacious Death of Father João, an "Unimportant" Man

Now it was on this wise that the martyrdom of the blessed João took place, a martyrdom efficacious for the raising to new life of a people who had, until such time as Father João gave his life for them, waxed fearful and remained embodiments of living death.

For in those times there was fear throughout the land. The people dared not raise their voices nor cry aloud to heaven for release from the heaviness of an oppression that the rulers laid upon them both day and night. When ruthless men came and took the lands whereon the peasants dwelt and ousted them by divers means from the soil of their forebears, there was not one to lift a voice on their behalf. And so the evil of their exploitation continued.

And when, after a father resisted the taking captive of his two beloved sons by a most barbarous officer, killing the officer in self-defense, behold, the police took his sister and daughter-in-law captive and beat them, inflicting all manner of cruel torture upon them. And when their cries became ever louder and their pleadings more importunate, a youth in the village, hearing their distress, went forthwith to the bishop, entreating him to intercede on their behalf. And straightway did the bishop go to the police station, taking with him the blessed João, a member of the Society of Jesus who pled to accompany his excellency on an errand of such justice and mercy.

So brutal were the police, who, without ceasing, were continuing to inflict cruel assaults on the women, that when Father João stated his intention to report the matter to the regional authorities,

Published in *The Other Side* (October 1986), pp. 16–18.

a soldier who was present smote him a blow on the face and shot him through the head straightway.

Father João made his peace with God and prepared to die. He assured those who sought in vain to assuage his wounds that he offered up his life and death for the people who had been wronged in that region and repeated several times, in recollection of his blessed Savior on the cross, the words, *Consummatum est,* "It is accomplished." After three hours, he lost consciousness. The next day he died.

And the people, who until now had been fearful to speak their indignation at acts of perfidy against their kind, did now wax wondrously indignant at the death of Father João and were not accepting of it. And behold, at the seventh-day mass to honor the memory of the slain priest, their indignation overflowed, and, lamenting the evil that had been their lot, they marched in great solidarity to the site of his murder and of the torture of the two women, and there they planted a cross as a memorial. Then some, no longer willing to accept their lot, shouted out their wrath. "This is not a place where justice has been done," some said. "This is not a place where justice *can* be done." And together they acted out their wrath, destroying with their hands and fists and shovels and axes the police station, after which they broke down the walls of the jail and freed the prisoners, responding to the mandate of their Lord to liberate the captives.

And when there was no longer stone upon stone in that place, only the cross remained—a cross of suffering, of judgment, of triumph. And they proclaimed that Father João was yet alive in them and that in their action they were taking on the burden of his mission. And behold, they felt themselves empowered as from on high to continue in the struggle for the liberation of the oppressed as Father João had done and his Lord had done before him.

And the governors of the realm did hear of these actions and the actions of divers others elsewhere. And it came to pass that they enacted laws that forbade torture. And thus it was that Father João's death was efficacious for the ongoing life of many others and remains so to this day.

That's the way we like our martyrs. Neat. Clear. Archaic. Miracle plays set in the distant past, surrounded by enough quaintness of language that they can be kept back there without intruding into our modern, logically structured world. We envision martyrs as those Christians going to the lions; early church fathers and mothers being stoned, sawed in two, killed with the sword; medieval saints gladly forsaking this world for the sake of another; Joan of Arc.

We can handle such tales without being terribly upset. Fortunately, we reflect, that kind of price is not exacted any longer for Christian witness; some inconvenience perhaps, a fine, even a short jail sentence (for which we get heavenly points)—but not violent death, not torture. Right? Wrong.

The story reproduced above is not a transcription from an ancient manuscript. It didn't even take place in a distant hemisphere—in eastern Europe, say, where people are laboring, so we are told, under communist oppression. It happened in our own hemisphere, in Brazil. The priest was João Bosco Burnier, a Jesuit. The bishop was Pedro Casaldaliga, bishop of São Felix, whose own life has been the object of numerous death threats. The town was Ribeirão Bonito. The date was October 11, 1976. Nor was it the last such death in Latin America. There have been more than seventy thousand civilian deaths since then in El Salvador alone. There are more, throughout Latin America and the impoverished world, every day.

What does this story tell us about our world? Many things, but these at least among them:

The killing of innocents does not occur only when a priest is shot or two women are tortured. The killing is built into the very structures of the life of the people—economic exploitation, political repression, military domination. Violence defines them all. Land is taken from those who have worked it to feed their families, and the crops that sustained the people are replaced by export crops such as coffee, which will not fill the stomachs of starving children. For every act of overt violence and torture, such as the story of João Bosco Burnier, there is the ongoing "hidden violence" (hidden from all but its victims) that occurs everyday when children starve, men cannot find work, women die in childbirth, and dignity is destroyed.

Sometimes it takes an immediate event, such as the shooting of Burnier, to surface the pent-up feelings of those who have been dispossessed and to kindle in them the feeling of "No more!" We will never understand what went on in Ribeirão Bonito if we dwell only on the immediate event. Centuries of exploitation and oppression surface in the decision to destroy a police station or a jail cell.

Such acts have consequences. The empowerment of people to take their destiny into their own hands is an important part of the tale. So is the fact that, because of this and similar acts elsewhere, the government of Brazil began to realize that acts of torture would not only harm the tortured but work finally against the torturers as well. It soon enacted laws to abolish torture as a legal instrument of the state. That does not mean that torture is no more, but from now on officials can no longer torture with impunity. From the vantage point of North American comfort, the distinction may seem academic. To a potential victim, however, the distinction is life-giving and fear-destroying.

The present moment is a time for the remembrance and celebration of the martyrdom of João Bosco Burnier. Just as his death served as a catalyst for the people of Ribeirão Bonito, it must serve as an ongoing catalyst for us. Just as Burnier's gospel commitment led him to be a "history maker," so too we must realize our capacity to change history and the direction of our societies. There is much torture still be be exposed, challenged, and eradicated. There is also—and this is harder—the need for contemporary counterparts of João who will embody the concept of the intervener against torture.

What does the story teach us about ourselves? Perhaps most of all, Burnier's martyrdom reminds us that we have a heritage. We are part of a long story, a rich past. We are surrounded, as the epistle to the Hebrews reminds us, by "a cloud of witnesses," and their story, as that same epistle also tells us, becomes *our* story. In the times in which we live, one part of the story that needs special highlighting is the account of those who side with the oppressed, who take on themselves the cause, and even the plight, of the victims.

In his living protest against torture and oppression, Burnier was recapitulating the story of Bartolomé de las Casas who, almost five centuries earlier, had taken on the lonely task of being the advocate of the Indians against the ruthless pillaging and killing of the Spanish conquistadores. We still have our conquistadores today, even if they are no longer Spanish, and the need for solidarity with their victims continues. The struggle takes many forms in many places. We recall, for example, the deliberate attempt of a "civilized" nation to destroy an entire people, the Jews. One "good" that has come out of that unmitigated evil has been the willingness of the Jews to affirm and thank the "righteous Gentiles," those who, not being Jews, nevertheless made it their task to hide, transport, and save Jews whenever possible, always at risk to themselves.

The indignities against which our heritage is called to stand today include the practice of torture. Torture is never justified, and tales of its practice, such as this one, must energize us to find ways to make its repetition impossible. The cry of the Jews after the torture of Auschwitz became "Never again!" So too in Brazil, reflection on torture has led to a massive report, *Brasil: Nunca Mais* (Brazil: Never Again).

Such is the power of the gospel that *a death-story can become a resurrection-story*. A priest dies, a people is resurrected—good news. His dying leads to their being raised from a living death. Their journey from fear to courage is a significant journey—perhaps the longest journey of which the human spirit, by grace, is capable. There is a commitment to make of João's death not an end but a beginning. As Bishop Pedro Casaldaliga says, "Blood is always a commitment." João, in his dying moments, realizes that in some sense he is replicating the story of Calvary; the cry of Jesus, "It is finished," is one that João makes his own.

The death of Jesus is unique and once-for-all. But in a world whose very structure has been changed by that death, Jesus' followers have no lack of opportunity to replicate something of the meaning of his death. Why, otherwise, would he have issued an invitation to his followers to take up their own crosses?

We will always need the reminder of Jesus' death as the visible enactment of the measure and cost of God's love for us. Nonetheless, we must work for a society that will not need an endless succession of martyrs in order to galvanize us into action for justice. João Bosco Burnier's death galvanized his friends, and it can so galvanize us. But his work will not be done until there is no need for further deaths like his and until all of us have taken his vocation upon ourselves.

Part 4.
A Broader and Deeper Ecumenism

Words have histories. Originally the Greek word *oikoumene* (from which we get "ecumenism") simply meant "the inhabited world," or "where the folks have gathered." It was preempted in early Christian history to represent the church, wherever it might be in the *oikoumene*. When Christians from all over the world would gather to debate the faith, the event was an "ecumenical" council.

And then, for a long time, people fought over the idea or ignored it. It got blown to smithereens in the sixteenth century as multitudes of Christians divided and redivided into denominations. But by the nineteenth century it was agreed in principle that disunity was a bad thing and that it should be overcome. It hasn't been easy.

That's about where things stand today. The emphasis is on getting together again, and church union (more properly "re-union") is center stage but *only with a new twist*. For the church has reincorporated the decision to take seriously the entire inhabited world, the true *oikoumene*. Once more we recognize that division—all kinds of division such as class and race—must be overcome. The word for this concern is "secular ecumenism," which sounds like an oxymoron, but it is really where the action is. So the sequence of chapters that follow represents something of the spread that ecumenism today embodies:

> talking with strangers,
> affirming with Jews,
> doing ecology,
> trying a new-style "evangelism," encompassed by homey analogies like cookbooks.

"Broader," yes, but "deeper" also, for despite their diversity, all people share in a developing unity that is truly part of *this* world as well. Within diversity all are part of a developing unity. Speed the day.

17 New Ground Rules for Ecumenical Exchange

"Multiculturalism" is a long word with a short history. But it presents a new attitude that all of us are called upon to acknowledge and exemplify. It affirms that our religious orientation, whatever it is, is influenced by, even formed by, the particular cultural reality within which we live, think, and worship.

This has always been true, but overt acknowledgment of its truth has been a long time in coming. The result of this acknowledgment raises many more problems than it initially solves, and I want to suggest nine ways we can begin to work on a number of such problems together.

1. *The giving up of humanly definable absolutes.* This is not a coy way of saying that there are no absolutes, or that if there are, we should ignore them. It is simply a recognition that whatever we know about Them, or It, or He, or She (to employ some culturally conditioned pronouns for deity) is such a far cry from the real thing that we are not entitled to claim very much for our wisdom. It is folly to equate the divine with our understanding of the divine. I am advocating a modest theology that is quite prepared to concede that old ways of speaking or visualizing may need drastic overhaul, and that we need all the help we can get from all quarters.

2. *The surrender of the axiom that my tradition automatically has better insights than your tradition.* This is a safeguard against fanaticism as well as pride. If I have the whole truth, that means you do not, and since fidelity to the truth means the suppression

Portions of a talk given at the dedication of the Multicultural Institute at the Franciscan School of Theology in Berkeley, California, on May 8, 1993.

of untruth, I am entitled to dispose of your ideas (and even of you) if necessary. This was the classic defense of the Inquisition, whether practiced in Madrid, Geneva, or Salem, Massachusetts.

3. *The importance of dialogue without hidden agendas.* "Dialogue" is rightly an important word in all ecumenical situations, but it often means different things to its practitioners. The chief hidden agenda of a certain kind of dialogue is the desire to convert: "If I can just get things going the right way, my dialogue partners will see the rightness of my position and the wrongness of theirs." I remember a Catholic poster in the early years of the Week of Prayer for Christian Unity that showed the whole world streaming into Saint Peter's Basilica in Rome—an interpretation of the consequences of dialogue that did little to mollify Protestant fears of a hostile takeover.

4. *Recognizing the cultural trappings* in which all convictions are clothed, especially our own. There is no sacred book that is not in part the product of what its culture contributed to its development. Rather than apologize for our cultural differences and downplay them, we ought to give them center stage, for we have much to learn from the various cultural dimensions of the idea, the book, the dance, the painting, the sculpture, the song.

5. *The importance of starting with each other.* Whatever our cultural background, we all share a common humanity across cultural differences—students and teachers alike. We can begin by celebrating this common humanity, and sharing whatever parts of our culture illumine that humanity for us. We do not start with a full complement of eternal truths to dispense to one another. (If we do, communication is going to get clogged early in the process.) Let us remember the definition of D. T. Niles, a World Council of Churches pioneer, that evangelism is "one begger telling another begger where to find bread." We will be helped in this process by recognizing the importance in theological communication of the role of *story*. We can share stories long before we can share theories of atonement. That the stories are always wrapped in cultural garments is a further plus: As we understand the other story we come also to understand the other culture. Gain all around.

118

6. We need to *receive help from others, not just impart help to others.* We in the West are so ready to give advice and counsel, especially when it gives us a sense of psychological or moral superiority. We need to turn the scriptural admonition around, and realize that sometimes "it is more blessed to receive than to give." Our penchant to jump in and explain things transforms the likelihood of degrading dialogue into strident monologue. We also enact the academician's familiar posture of giving a brilliant answer to a question that has not been asked.

7. We need to *learn about other cultures and faiths from their practitioners,* not from our own interpreters. During my college days in the 1940s a spate of books appeared about "the world's great religions," all written by Christians and all demonstrating, after a series of comparisons, that Christianity was far superior to all the others in such categories as its view of God, God's relation to the world, and comparative schemes of redemption. Such an approach has no place in the future. We are not engaging in a religious sweepstakes to see who wins, places, and shows. We are trying to get to know one another better. We are trying to have our own faith enriched by drawing on one another's resources.

8. *We need to do things together* in order to learn who we really are. As liberation theologian Gustavo Gutiérrez has pointed out, theology is always the "second act." The first act is commitment—to one another and especially to the disadvantaged. We work together, we think together, and—this is new for many—we celebrate together. We discover who we are, not just in head trips, but in walking together, on previously untrodden paths, maybe even dancing on the way. We find each other both in projects designed to create social justice and in fiestas that remind us that we can share the bounty of creation even in the midst of sorrow and heavy responsibilities.

9. Finally, we recognize that *all these matters have desperate urgency.* If you doubt that, think for a moment about Bosnia and what is going on there even as we organize study groups to talk about Bosnia. The problem in Bosnia is precisely that so many people cannot yet handle multiculturalism. They are determined to blow out the brains of people who disagree or come from a different cultural background. "Ethnic cleansing" becomes

a norm for action—an obscene criterion. In such situations, the issues for many are life and death, whereas most of us can talk together, play together, work together, without fear. It is an extraordinary privilege. In our own less harassed, but still confused, lives, all these matters call for attention, and especially for openness. New ideas often frighten us and make us more rigid than we need or ought to be. We will have to trust our dialogue partners, remembering all the while that the best way to elicit trust is to exemplify it. If we can keep that theme uppermost, we can approach the most complex issues in hope rather than fear.

18 The Baleful Role of Non-Jews in the Holocaust

"If the victims are my problem," Elie Wiesel once said to a group of Christians, "the killers are yours." This assessment has the power of being true as well as blunt. *The victims are* a problem for Jews: Why were Jews singled out to be Hitler's scapegoats? Where was the God of Sinai, of Abraham and Sarah, of Amos and Deborah, when six million of God's people, including over a million children, were being exterminated? What does it take to bring the Messiah, if six million deaths are not enough?

But *the killers* are our problem, the problem of non-Jews and especially Christians. For it was a culture deeply permeated by "Christian Values" and the Christian church, that created and implemented the Final Solution. Nazi guards turned vicious dogs on Jewish children on Saturdays and received Holy Communion on Sundays. Christians who said the creed in church said another creed, "Heil Hitler!" on the city streets. With few exceptions, those in the churches preferred not to know what was going on, or gave their approval to what was going on; after all, hadn't the Jews rejected Christ, the redeemer of the world?

In the face of the Holocaust, the first thing we Christians have to do is acknowledge our culpability, not only in the near success of the Final Solution, but in the centuries of Christian anti-Semitism that paved the way for it. Holocaust scholar Raul Hilberg has compressed that history into three devastating sentences. The first is "*Jews have no right to live among us as Jews,*" and the consequent action was the attempt to convert. The second was a little shorter, and came in the Middle Ages: "*Jews have no right to live among*

Originally given as a speech at a Holocaust memorial service at Carleton College, Northfield, Minnesota, in March 1987.

us," and the consequent action was the ghetto, forcing Jews into totally separate places of habitation. The third was shorter still: "*Jews have no right to live,*" and the consequence of that conviction was the Final Solution, the creation of the death camps for the express purpose of killing Jews. The way the Christian faith was interpreted in Germany helped to pave the way for all that, and no amount of trying to ignore that fact will finally succeed.

Only after we have pondered long and hard on that reality are we entitled to say, for a moment, "But there were some exceptions." It is true; there *were* some exceptions: Martin Niemoeller, a Lutheran pastor who spent seven years in a concentration camp; Roman Catholic Bishop Lichtenberger, who spoke out when it was dangerous to do so; Father Delp, S.J., who died in the camps; Dietrich Bonhoeffer, who said, "Only those who cry out for the Jews have the right to sing Gregorian chant," and who participated in the plot against Hitler's life and was hanged for it. When you go to Yad Vashem in Jerusalem, the great place of remembrance, you encounter what is called the Avenue of the Righteous Gentiles, a street, as yet unfinished, lined with trees, each one of which is a memorial to a non-Jew who risked his or her own life to save Jews. Yes, there were exceptions.

But they were so few . . . Our temptation is to let the few who had integrity stand for the rest of us. And we cannot do that. The most we can do is persuade ourselves that they were the ones who acted truly out of the faith we share, and that the others—the vast multitudes—betrayed both the Jews and the faith we share. That will not change the facts. But it may change what we do with the facts.

I do not believe that anti-Semitism is endemic to Christian faith, though I know there is a lot in the Christian track record that persuades others that it is so. If it is an aberration, and if failing to stand by others in their time of need is an aberration, then once we have acknowledged the reality of the complicity of Christians in horrible events of the past, we must make it our project, for the present and the future, to see that clearer understandings of our faith prevail, and that we act more courageously on the basis of these understandings.

At Treblinka, the death camp outside Warsaw, where Nazi efficiency was so perfected that fifteen thousand people a day could be gassed and their bodies burned, you come finally to a huge monument, near which, carved in six languages, is a single legend that in English reads, "Never again."

That is the lesson we all need to learn from the events of the Nazi era. That is the good we must seek to wrest out of the unmitigated evil, that although these things happened once, never again must they be permitted to happen. Never again must anyone, Jew or non-Jew, adult or child, man or woman, be treated as an object rather than a person, made expendable for the sake of an ideology, subjected to fear of being taken off in the middle of the night, shipped in a cattle car to a destination unknown, and treated as absolutely worthless and discardable. Never again.

That is why the story needs to continue being told. There are people today who are, as they put it, "tired" of hearing about the Holocaust. Seal off the past, they say, look to the future; do not wallow in past misdeeds; create future good deeds. But they are wrong. As philosopher George Santayana put it, "Those who forget history are doomed to repeat it." We "forgot" the Holocaust, so Vietnam and Nicaragua resulted. Some people in the White House forgot Watergate, and Irangate resulted. If we again forget Auschwitz, before we know it there will be a new Auschwitz. We must hear the story again and again, precisely because it was not beasts or identifiably immoral monsters who created Auschwitz. Rather, it was good, decent citizens, heirs of the legacy of Goethe and Schiller, Beethoven and Mahler, the trained scientists who used their skills for evil ends—people like us—the cream of the crop, who were architects of the Final Solution. What a blow it was to my own college undergraduate perspective about how education could save us all from folly, to learn that Josef Goebbels, Hitler's minister of propaganda, had a Ph.D.

Jews will help us remember Auschwitz. They were there. Those who survived were permanently scarred by what happened there. There is no European Jew living who did not have a relative who died in the death camps. They will help us remember.

But the message non-Jews need to hear today is that *we* must remember also. Jews can only remember with pain; we can only remember with shame. And the only way we can begin to deal with the shame is to persuade the world that what we were involved in then was an aberration of who we truly are, rather than an example of who we truly are. And that message will be communicated not chiefly by words but mainly by deeds. Whenever there is the first tiny whisper of anti-Semitism, anywhere, we must say, "Never again." Whenever any child is ridiculed or neglected, as so many are today, we must say, "Never again." Whenever any people begins to say, "We are the ones who should rule the world!" we must say, "Never again." Whenever a politician whispers, "Oh, but those people aren't as important as we are, so that if some of them don't survive, that doesn't really matter," we must say, "Never again." Whenever someone says, "Six million dead in a nuclear attack is an acceptable loss," we must say, "Never again."

We will never erase the history of the years 1933 to 1945 from the rest of human history. It will always remain an evil stain on the annals of humanity. But we can at least learn from it and, by keeping the story alive, seek to ensure that finally the entire human family will join in the refrain, "Never again."

19 Theology and Ecology
From a Destructive Past to a Constructive Future

In the third world, don't drink the water.
In the first world, don't breathe the air.
—the wisdom of the twentieth century

To harm the earth is to heap contempt upon
its creator.
   —the wisdom of the nineteenth century,
     in the words of Chief Seattle

The words "ecology," "ecumenism," and "economics" share both a linguistic and a substantive connection. The linguistic connection is that they all grow out of the original Greek word *eikos,* meaning house or habitation. The substantive connection is that they are all concerned with how various "households" collaborate, *economics* dealing with the relationships between people in terms of fiscal interaction, *ecumenism* dealing with their interrelationships both as dwellers in "the inhabited world" and as part of the divine society, and *ecology* dealing with the relationship of all living organisms (whether human or not) to their environment.

The interrelationships are more frequently noted in the breach than in the observance: economists are not terribly attracted to ecumenists and vice versa, and neither of them have, until recently, factored care for the environment into an understanding of their respective disciplines.

Such studied independence will no longer work, and the concept of "eco-justice" is an attempt to make things work better, to build bridges and forge links. Both economists and ecumenists (or as we shall now say, "theologians") are now required to take account not only of each other but of ecology as well. We shall concentrate here on how those who stand within the religious tradition, and particularly within the Christian tradition, can begin to wed ecology and theology.

Any rapprochement between eco-justice and theology must start with a communal *mea culpa* on the part of Christians. We have not only neglected to include the care of the earth within our ecclesiastical and personal agendas, but that very neglect has worked positive hardship, for such neglect is never benign but only destructive. To do nothing has meant to make things worse.

Most theological discussions begin by acknowledging the charges leveled against the church by educator Lynn White, in a famous essay, "The Historical Roots of Our Ecological Crisis."[1] White charges that the biblical perspective has permitted, and even encouraged, human beings to *dominate* nature for purely human ends, whether such actions were supportive of the earth or not.[2]

White's essay asserts flatly that "Christianity bears a huge burden of guilt" for the ecological crisis in which we find ourselves. From the eighteenth and nineteenth centuries to the present, scientific and technological breakthroughs have allowed human beings to exploit the earth for quick financial gain, with no thought about the long-term consequences of such actions. Christianity's reliance on the Genesis creation stories, particularly the emphasis on human beings having "dominion" over the earth and its creatures, made it possible to treat the earth as if it were created exclusively for the "use" of human beings, with no concern for the consequences, so that "use" soon came to mean "exploitation." White encapsulates the approach as follows:

> God planned all of [this earth] explicitly for human benefit and rule; no item in the physical creation had any purpose save to serve humanity's needs.[3]

There was no notion of the sacrality of nature in this view, as there had been, for example, in primitive animistic cultures that displayed a high regard for the whole of creation. So instead of reverencing nature, human beings soon felt free to abuse it for personal gain, and have done so ever since.

The Crisis

The extent of the resultant crisis is now menacingly widespread, as a few examples will indicate. Here is a sampling of ills that theologian/farmer

Richard Austin notes: acid rain and toxic pollution, ozone depletion, the "greenhouse effect," rain forest destruction, desertification, mineral depletion, population explosion, the threat of nuclear war.[4]

Another detailed accounting with very little overlap is offered in *Keeping and Healing the Creation,* a 1989 report of a Presbyterian ecojustice task force: the destruction of renewable foods, erosion of croplands, diminishing yields at fisheries, exhaustion of nonrenewable minerals, acidification of the atmosphere, global warming, ozone depletion, diminishment of water supplies, unhealthy disposal of hazardous wastes, extinction of various forms of nonhuman life, genetic experiments on domestic animals.[5]

What this translates into is that there are scarcely any areas of the planet, any forms of life on the planet, or any nonliving objects on the planet that are not in one way or another threatened by ongoing active exploitation by members of the human species.

If one wants more compelling evidence than a further compiling of lists, the opening paragraphs of Alan Paton's *Cry, the Beloved Country* provide a heart-rending example of how the original beauty of the earth has been ravaged by rapacious men (the sexist language is, for once, appropriate).[6] Paton describes how an area of South Africa, once a place of beauty and fecundity, has been transformed into a place of ugliness and barrenness — the world of nature denuded of its loveliness and living under a curse rather than a promise, as a consequence of the oppressive and manipulative activity of human beings.

The same dynamics are further amplified and rendered even more poignant in Paton's later book, *Ah, but Your Land Is Beautiful.* The title is a phrase Paton often heard on the lips of visitors to South Africa. It had two meanings: (1) the land is beautiful when people do not despoil it, and (2) it is particularly beautiful in comparison to the ugly patterns of *apartheid* that people have imposed upon it. In South Africa, Paton tells us throughout his writing, one cannot finally separate the sins of human nature *against* nature itself (eco-injustice) from the sins committed *within* human nature (social injustice). The two belong together: eco-justice must include concern for humanity as well as the earth, while social justice must include concern for the earth as well as for humanity.

A Broader and Deeper Ecumenism

As we deal with this theme theologically, it is clear that two separate and yet interlocked concerns must be kept in mind: (1) "the implications of the eco-justice crisis for the ongoing reconstruction of theology," and (2) "the contributions of theology to understanding the crisis and responding faithfully to it."[7] It is impossible, however, to keep these two concerns separate. At every point they interact with each other. Reciprocal dealings are at work here: Theology needs to be re-created by entering into the world of eco-justice concerns that it has heretofore passively ignored or actively shunned. The eco-crisis needs to be viewed from theological as well as other vantage points.

Some Interconnections

Further comments about the relationship between the cognates *ecology* and *economics* will help clarify issues. It is clear that economic interests have guided much of the exploitation of the world of nature at the hand of human nature. Early in his exploration of these themes, John Muir blamed capitalism for much of the denuding of the forests in the West with no initial regard for reseeding or selective cutting. The desire for a quick profit far outweighed concern for the long-range consequences of that desire.

Thomas Berry, a Roman Catholic leader in environmental courses, employing language drawn from the realm of economics, characterizes our wasting of natural resources as an example of "deficit expenditure."[8] In simplest terms this means that we use up much more of the natural order than we replace. Sun, water, soil, forests, and oceans are all degraded, and we create, in an image Berry frequently uses, a "wasteland" rather than a "wonderland." The examples given earlier of the mounting ecological crisis are instances of deficit expenditure. Failure to take account of the long-range consequences of our present actions means that unless or until reverse measures are adopted, the crisis will only deepen.

To put the clearest and least ambiguous face on it, what we are dealing with here is the widespread human characteristic of *greed,* an energy that has powered most human economic activity. One of the characteristics of greed is wanting something so badly that the eventual negative consequences of getting it are subordinated to the immediate gratification. Greed does not remain within containable limits; when an immediate satisfaction has been achieved, it is transformed into a stepping-stone toward the fulfillment of yet greater desires. Those who stand in the way will be ruthlessly pushed aside, those whose superior gratifications have already been met will be first envied, then challenged, and whenever possible, overthrown. In the process, both nature and human nature become objects to be manipulated. Injustices are committed against both human beings and the environment they inhabit.[9]

A new sort of analysis is called for, and the perspective of liberation theology offers help. It has been one of the insistent themes of liberation theology that there are manifold injustices in the economic order that work against the poor, the oppressed, and the victims, and that call for concerned and unified action by the victims themselves. What is now becoming clear, and is of great importance to the liberation struggle, is "the great new insight of our time"—that *nature has become co-victim with the poor,* that the vulnerable earth and the vulnerable people are oppressed together. It has become necessary to understand human justice as eco-justice. "The 'eco' for ecology suggests that the urgent ecological problems are connected with the more traditional concern for social and economic justice."[10]

This is not the discovery of a new fact, but repossession of an old fact that goes back to biblical times: "The biblical memory of liberation includes not just oppressed people, but also oppressed lands."[11] People need not only inter-human justice but eco-justice. The goal of the children of Israel in their wandering was not just the promise of better inter-human relationships, but the promised *land.* Jesus' location in the social structures of the ancient world helps to reinforce this; he was not one of the landed aristocracy, nor did he come from a well-connected "political family"; he was a Jew, and furthermore he was one of the *am-ha'aretz,* the poor of the land, whose very survival depended on rootage in the soil and access to its nourishment.

This reinforced recognition of the interrelationships of nature and human nature is writ large in the plight of the poor. It is not enough that they receive a better deal within the economic order; there must be similar guarantees within the ecological order as well. Indiscriminate cutting of the

Brazilian rain forests not only affects weather conditions in other parts of the globe but renders habitation for the poor in Brazil increasingly hazardous. To the degree that the rich nations let global warming proceed unchecked at the polar ice caps, the consequent rise in the sea level will threaten the inhabitants of islands in the South Pacific not only with loss of their livelihood but their very survival as well. Attempts by first-world countries to dump toxic wastes in remote Pacific islands (or remote places on various land masses) will increasingly befoul the earth and the atmosphere, and make human habitation adjacent to those areas not only increasingly problematic but finally impossible.

Unfortunately, impulses to greed and consequent ecological disaster will not be overcome by goodwill on the part of a few, or moral exhortations addressed to the miscreants. What is needed is increasing legislation not only in regional but in global terms. There is a need for increasing pressure and lobbying in all the decision-making chambers of the human family, and for taking punitive action against those who will not comply with new and increasingly stringent legislation.

The Interrelationship of Nature and Human Nature

To complement assaults on the injustice of existing social, political, and economic structures, we need fresh thinking about how human minds and human hearts work. Systemic change and individual change need as much linkage as possible, so that nature and human nature can be partners rather than competitors.

Those who are uncomfortable with the disastrous separation of nature and human nature, to which Lynn White's essay calls attention, need to be reminded that in the creation stories "Adam" is not a proper name for a masculine individual. The Hebrew *adham* refers to humanity-as-relationship, using the explicit example of male-and-female-in-relationship. It is this fact of relationship that leads the authors of the Genesis accounts to describe this human relationship as the primary image of the nature of God. But what has often been forgotten is that humanity-as-relationship is not only human beings in relationship to one another but in relationship to the *earth* as well, for *adham* derives from the Hebrew word *adhamah,* which means "earth." *Adham* and *adhamah* are intertwined, not separated. This linkage between nature and human nature is thus not something new, but the rediscovery of something old and enduring. Any dualisms, particularly those that claim biblical authority for allowing *adham* to subdue, control, and manipulate *adhamah,* thus need to be challenged.

Humanity does not stand, therefore, as separate, and above, and consequently in control of the order of nature, but as part of it, not to exploit but to care for and nurture it.

The consequences of this connection are recognized in a recent creedal statement of the Presbyterian Church (U.S.A.), in which the concept of sin is extended from individual peccadilloes to an acknowledgment of corporate violations of God's will for humankind, not only as exploitation of "neighbor" but as exploitation of "nature" as well. By such exploitation, the creed reminds us, we "threaten death to the planet entrusted to our care."

This may be the first specific treatment of ecological issues in the history of creed making, although the idea of linking sin to the exploitation of the earth goes back at least as far as Jeremiah:

> This people has a rebellious and defiant heart . . .
> They did not say to themselves,
>> "Let us fear the Lord our God,
>> who gives us the rains of autumn,
>> and spring showers in their turn,
>> who brings us unfailingly
>> fixed seasons of harvest."
> But *your wrongdoing has upset nature's order*
> and your sins have kept from you her kindly gifts.[12]

The issue of our relationship to the natural order deserves fuller examination, and help is available from noted Jewish thinker Abraham Joshua Heschel.[13] There are three ways, he writes, in which we may respond to the created order: "We may exploit it, we may enjoy it, we may accept it with awe."[14]

That we have *exploited* the earth is patent. That we can *enjoy* it is a creative possibility open to us, and is an advance over exploitation, but it is still possible, in a blind-sided kind of enjoyment, to continue its exploitation, whether consciously or not. The truly mature attitude, Heschel insists, in which we can avoid debasing not only the created order but those who live within it, is to accept the created order with *awe*. This leads to an attitude of "radical amazement." And radical amazement, to Heschel, leads us to see that the world in which we are placed is not self-explanatory but a sheer gift of God to be seen—the more so now—as something infinitely precious, and therefore in need of the most lavish sort of care.

Hard-line Protestants are frequently suspicious of such a line of argument, fearing that it will lead to some kind of nature-mysticism or even a form of pantheism. The suspicion cannot be dismissed out of hand; there *have* been those who confused God and God's creation, but the danger in the opposite direction, of reducing the created order to a subordinate status and failing to safeguard it against both theological and ecological abuse, would seem at present to be greater.

If we affirm something with reverential awe, with wonder, with radical amazement, we are less likely to subject it to callous manipulation and consequent destruction than if we are simply dealing with material stuff out there that can consequently be viewed as fair game for exploitation.

A further insight from Heschel offers a safeguard from any demeaning of the earth or neglect of it. Heschel points out that in the Hebrew scriptures the word *eretz* (earth) occurs five times as often as the word *shamayim* (heaven).[15] Consequently, we may not dismiss the earth as of only passing importance to God and God's creatures. Poetic insight to the contrary notwithstanding, earth is not *just* Keats's "vale of soul-making," and thus of only transitory concern. It has a final worth in its own right and must be treated as such. Heaven is not the center of attention in the Scriptures; earth is, and earth must consequently be treated with great care and love. Any neglect or despoliation of the earth, or life on earth, flies in the face of the preciousness with which earth is viewed in the sight of God.[16]

Having examined the relationship of nature and human nature from the side of humanity, we can now consider a broader view of the created order in its totality.

It has been customary in such discussion to view the goodness of creation as the starting point, a creation into which human beings were subsequently inserted with disastrous results. But new expressions of theological method coming to us chiefly from the third world make it more compelling to begin where two European theologians, Ulrich Duchrow and Gerhard Liedke, suggest we must begin with God saying not, "Behold, it was very good" (Genesis 1:31) but "Behold, it was very corrupt" (Genesis 6:12).

> The point of departure for a theology of creation today can no longer be the goodness of creation in which God's goodness is reflected. The point of departure for us can only be the suffering of creation: the inordinate suffering caused by the modern growth in human violence against non-human creation, the suffering that makes the chasm of sin through creating excruciatingly painful."[17]

From this perspective, it will never be possible to think about nature and human nature save together. From our first exploration, we will be aware of what we have done to creation and the degree to which we therefore inherit responsibility for working toward its re-creation. This makes even more significant the close relationship between God and creation and the Christian claim that God loves the world—even the world that God's children have so abused—and most significant of all that God continues to love the creatures who have put such a crimp on the divine plan. This means also that traditional theologies that center on the doctrine of redemption to the almost complete exclusion of the meaning of creation (save as a kind of stage set for the *real* story, i.e., human emancipation from sin) will be unable to tell their story apart from the mess that human beings have made of the creation. The redemption of humanity and the redemption of the entire created order will be one intertwined story rather than two separate ones, as has been so true in the past.

A further way to trace the intertwining will be a recognition that instead of creation being important only where it impinges on the life and destiny of humanity, creation as a whole will have to be affirmed. At the end of the sixth day of creation, it is reported that "God saw *everything* that [God] had made, and behold, it was very good" (Genesis 1:31, italics added). Ecological concern will only proceed responsibly if a similarly generous view of the lasting significance of every aspect of the created order is restored to center stage. Otherwise, humanity will blunder into the twenty-first century still seeking trade-offs with the natural order that will continue to render much of it expendable. Only if we are committed to the welfare of everything can we guarantee the survival of anything.

The Special challenges of Technology and Modern War

Along with ongoing concerns for a new balance between the human species and the environment, two recent challenges exacerbate the overall problem and need special attention: technology and modern war.

The first challenge, the ongoing impact of human *technology,* raises a question. Does it represent a boon to our culture, or is it a bane for ongoing life on the planet? From the earliest times, technology, in however primitive a form, has been part of human life. The "discovery of fire," the "invention" of the wheel, the use of hammer and saw, are all examples of technology that have made possible not only warmth, faster transportation, and furniture, but the creation of leisure time that makes culture possible. The downside, of course, has been that the technologies thus developed can be used for evil ends as well—fire can be an instrument of torture, the wheel (attached to a B-52) makes carpet bombing possible, and a hammer can be used to bludgeon an enemy's brains.

The morally ambiguous uses to which technological advances are subject have led some Christians to assess negatively their value to human society. Leonardo da Vinci, so it is reported, drew plans for a rudimentary submarine but (with remarkable prescience) never shared them in his lifetime, for fear that greedy profiteers would use the submarine in warfare to subdue an enemy.

The logical outworking of such reservations came to a head at the initial assembly of the World Council of Churches in Amsterdam in 1948, when one proposed document sharply criticized the dehumanizing role of technology in modern life. At that point Rajah Manikam, a delegate from India, rose and said to the delegates, "Before you condemn technology, would you let us have it, please, in India, for fifty years?"

It is clear that the more advanced technology becomes, the greater threat it poses to the ecosystem. Here Thomas Berry's concept of "deficit expenditure" receives its most deadly application. It is not simply that various raw materials are drawn from the earth and refined for other purposes than those for which they were created, but that the wastes that are created in, say, a nuclear power plant are so destructive that there is as yet no way known to contain them and keep them from polluting the earth, the rivers and oceans, and the atmosphere. The extraordinary shortsightedness of creating materials of destructive power that are themselves unable to be destroyed is only one instance of how the baleful effect of technology on the environment has taken a quantum leap within our own lifetimes.

Another example illustrates the interplay between refined instruments of technology and the baleful effect on human existence. No matter to what extent manufacturing and assembly plants are automated, a human work force is still needed. Many U.S. corporations have developed "border industries," *maquiladores,* in which a significant part of the manufacture of a U.S. product is done outside the country. Human nature is abused in the low wages paid, lack of healthful working conditions, and prohibition against organizing, establishing trade unions, and so forth. But in the absence of environmental standards in the third-world countries where the work is done, not only do workers inhale almost lethal doses of toxic fumes, but the environment itself is badly polluted, either through what goes out of the chimneys or what is dumped into the ground as raw, and very dangerous, sewage. Since the workers always live nearby, often in wretched housing, not only the air they breathe but the water they drink is almost sure to be contaminated.

In such situations, both nature and human nature are exploited. The only remedy will be strong legislation, and it will have to be done globally, or businesses will gravitate to those parts of the world where there are either no laws or nonenforcement of existing laws.

The second area that poses special problems to the relationship between humans and the environment is the case of *modern war*. All that I have said about technology applies here, of course, since it is the very nature of modern war to be more and more technologically waged. Especially if future warfare escalates into nuclear war, we will face not only massive loss of life, but radioactive fallout that will threaten the very possibility of continuing life on the planet. There is no way to combine care of the earth with nuclear capability.

When modern "advances" in weapons production now include the ability to wage chemical warfare and release poison gasses of extraordinary potency, we have another situation in which the destruction of nature and the destruction of human nature will occur simultaneously. We have already seen the destructive effect of Agent Orange, used in Vietnam, which was not only capable of destroying whole forests quickly, but whole battalions slowly, as the men who released the Agent Orange later developed cancer and other deadly reactions that led to their lingering deaths.

As the recent war in the Middle East has shown, further acts of the destruction of the ecosystem take place in time of war that would be unthinkable in time of peace, such as the deliberate creation of an oil spill in the Persian Gulf and the setting on fire of hundreds of Kuwaiti oil wells. The ecological harm of these two events alone will last for decades, and many of the losses to wildlife in the gulf will be irretrievable. And we are only beginning to discover that our own Gulf War veterans are suffering maladies that can be traced to the use of poison gas.

No one has devised a legislative process that can outlaw war. But it may be that the increasingly higher stakes for the planet's sheer survival in the face of vast eco-damage may begin to suggest new ways to deal with conflict resolution short of war. Whether the lesson can be learned before irreversible damage has been done is perhaps the most fateful conjecture of our time.

Jubilee:
A Framework for the Future

What are we to do about all this? The symbol that brings together both of these concerns is the biblical symbol of the Jubilee, referred to in Jesus' references to "the acceptable year of the Lord" as part of the agenda of his own ministry (Luke 4:16–30), and described in specific detail in Leviticus 25:1–23.[18]

The proposals for the Jubilee offer a series of radical opportunities for simultaneously reorienting persons to one another and to their environment.[19] Every seventh year the Hebrews were to let the earth lie fallow to enable it to regenerate, just as persons were to rest every seventh day for the same purpose. And every fiftieth year—the Jubilee—the earth was to lie fallow; all debts incurred since the previous Jubilee were to be canceled; all slaves bought in the interval were to be freed; and lands acquired since the previous Jubilee were to revert to their former owners, on the principle that the land was not the people's land but God's land, and therefore could not be sold in perpetuity.

It is not clear whether the provisions of the Jubilee ever made their way off the drawing board and into the actual lives of the people, but the Jubilee principle remained intact in the Hebrew scriptures, and Jesus made it part of the radical agenda for his own ministry (see Luke 4:16–20).

The symbol of the Jubilee is related to the concerns of eco-justice, particularly in two ways. First, *we are not to exploit the land.* This basic principle is built into the announcement that the land must lie fallow every seventh year and every fiftieth year so that it can be replenished, and further emphasized in the regulation that during every Jubilee the land will revert to its original owner so that huge exploitative landholdings cannot be accumulated by a few skillful entrepreneurs. Contemporary ecologists can spell out specific measures that are needed to save the earth in this and the next century and give it the care it deserves. In so doing, they will be contributing to the fulfillment of this part of the Jubilee mandate.

Second, *we are not to use the land to exploit people.* This is the clear import of several of the other Jubilee provisions. It will not be possible, for example, for a few persons with vested interests in the land to maintain control in perpetuity. Vast agribusiness holdings, for example, accumulated over half a century, will revert to their former owners, and a small-farm economy can be reintroduced.[20]

Moreover, the symbol of the Jubilee calls for *slaves to be freed.* Translated into our contemporary context, this would mean that those who work the land should be paid a living wage, thereby enabled to survive and thrive with dignity. And *debts are to be canceled,* providing once again that those with entrepreneurial skills will be prevented from locking others out of the economy.

Finally, this dream is *not to be deferred* to the far-distant future. It is to provide a series of regulations administered at least once during the lifetime of every citizen. Tomorrow is to come today.[21]

We thus see within the Jubilee provisions a clear link not only between person-and-person in the enactment of social justice but between persons-and-the-environment in the enactment of eco-justice. With whatever substantial adaptations are called for in the modern industrial era, Jubilee provides the symbolic content for a perspective that would radically alter not only the face of the earth but also the faces of the earth's inhabitants, to the mutual enrichment of each.

NOTES

1. Lynn White, "The Historical Roots of Our Ecological Crisis," *Science,* March 20, 1987: 1203–7.

2. See Richard Austin's *Beauty of the Lord,* page 2, and *Hope for the Land,* page 103. Austin's four volumes, which also include *Baptized into Wilderness* and *Reclaiming America* (Nashville: Creekside Press/Abingdon Press, 1987–1990), are among the most useful resources available on the subject of this paper.

3. Cited in Austin, *Hope for the Land,* 2, here rendered in inclusive language.

4. Ibid., 190–99.

5. *Keeping and Healing the Creation,* Eco-Justice Task Force, Committee on Social Witness Policy, Louisville, Ky., 1989, 5–42. An even more detailed accounting can be found in Ulrich Duchrow and Gerhard Liedke, *Shalom: Biblical Perspectives on Creation, Justice and Peace,* World Council of Churches, Geneva, 1989, pp. 15–35.

6. Alan Paton, *Cry, the Beloved Country* (New York: Charles Scribner's Sons, 1954).

7. *Keeping and Healing the Creation,* 45.

8. See Lonergan and Richards, eds., *Thomas Berry and the New Cosmology,* esp. 4–26, "Economics: Its Effect on the Life Systems of the World."

9. Ursula LeGuin, in *Always Coming Home* (New York: Harper & Row, 1985), describing a society in the future that has survived a cataclysm, offers a radically different way of seeing life. In the land of Kesh, the same noun can be translated into English as "wealth" and "generosity." She comments, "In such terms, people who don't own much because they keep giving things away are rich, while those who give little and so own much are poor" (p. 128).

10. *Keeping and Healing the Creation,* 58–59, italics added.

11. Austin, *Hope for the Land,* 4–5.

12. Jeremiah 5:23–25, New English Bible, cited in Austin, *Hope for the Land,* 169.

13. I have explored Heschel's thought in more detail in *Saying Yes and Saying No* (Philadelphia: Westminster Press, 1986), 47ff., and in Merkel, ed., *Abraham Joshua Heschel: Exploring His Life and Thought* (New York: Macmillan, 1985), chap. 8, "Some Are Guilty, All Are Responsible; Heschel's Social Ethics."

14. Abraham Joshua Heschel, *God in Search of Man* (New York: Farrar, Straus & Giroux, 1955), 34.

15. Abraham Joshua Heschel, *Israel: An Echo of Eternity* (New York: Farrar, Straus & Giroux, 1969).

16. An apparently remote theological problem also has relevance to the discussion. This is the problem, formalized in the medieval period, of *the relationship between nature and grace.*

What we call the Augustinian tradition has sharply separated the two: Man's sinful nature, deeply distorted by the Fall, can be redeemed not by gentle healing but only by a radical rupture with the past and a new beginning, the product not of human effort but solely of divine grace.

To the medieval understanding, however, nature and grace are less at odds with each other. Grace, rather than annihilating nature, fulfills or completes it. There is speaking and hearing distance between the two, rather than a chasm not bridgeable from the human side. This is because, in Thomas Aquinas and others, the consequences of the Fall are not so catastrophic. What is "lost" is the *donum superadditum,* the supernatural gifts without which human nature is still well endowed. The realm of nature remains a fertile field in which the seeds of grace may grow.

Classical Protestantism identified with the Augustinian rather than the Thomistic view: The utterly severed connections between nature and grace can be repaired only from the divine side of the broken relationship, by the sheer and unmerited gift of God.

However much these originally sharp distinctions may have been softened by the passage of time, connections between nature and human nature are easier to propose within some contemporary counterpart of the medieval view than within the Augustinian-Reformation view, since there remains a connection between the two that has not been totally destroyed. Such an observation is not meant to be a negation of classical Protestant theology, but rather a challenge to it, to formulate ways of relating nature and grace that will underline their intimate relationship rather than totally negating it. To see creation itself as a sheer gift, the supreme act of God's grace for the well-being of the entire human family, is an initial line of inquiry worth further exploration.

17. Duchrow and Liedke, *Shalom,* 47.

18. A full treatment of the Jubilee theme is in Ringe, Sharon, *Jesus, Liberation and the Biblical Jubilee* (Philadelphia: Fortress Press, 1985). Karen Lebacqz, in *Justice in an Unjust World* (Minneapolis: Augsburg, 1987), uses Jubilee as the controlling image in an important contribution to a Christian understanding of justice. See esp. chaps. 7–9. I have engaged in a briefer treatment in *Unexpected News: Reading the Bible with Third World Eyes,* (Philadelphia: Westminster, 1984), 88–104.

19. That the provisions for a Jubilee did not spring *de novo* from Leviticus 25 is made clear in Ringe's discussion of their two sources: (a) the Sabbath years laws (Ex. 21:2–6; 23:10–11; Deut. 15:1–18) and (b) the amnesty or "release" provisions set out in Jer. 34:18–22, and Neh. 5:1–13. See especially Ringe's chap. 2. Ringe also examines the New Testament passages where the themes are further developed, in addition to the *locus classicus,* Luke 4:16–30. See esp. chaps. 3–7.

20. Although he is not writing in the context of Jubilee concerns, Wendell Berry, in *The Unsettling of America: Culture and Agriculture* (San Francisco: Sierra Club Books, 1986), makes this case with power. See esp. chap. 2, "The Ecological Crisis as a Crisis of Character."

21. See Gutiérrez's treatment of this theme in Robert Brown, *Gustavo Gutiérrez* (Maryknoll, N.Y.: Orbis Books, 1990), 73–74.

20 From the Periphery to the Center
New Directions for What Used to Be Called "Evangelism"

Protestant church historian Kenneth Scott Latourette devoted many years of his life to writing a seven-volume history of the mission and expansion of Christianity—what today we call "evangelization."[1] He discovered that he had to devote an entire volume to what he called "The Great Century," which turned out to be the nineteenth. This was the time when European and North American Protestants put aside their intramural bickering and generated commitment and enthusiasm to take the good news of salvation across the seven seas, and to the four corners of the earth—two images that are extraordinarily lacking in descriptive accuracy but indicate at least the boundless extent of the endeavor.

In the early twentieth century, the Student Volunteer Movement concentrated its efforts on U.S. campuses and recruited missionaries galore under the banner of "the evangelization of the world in this generation."[2] Leaders like John R. Mott and Sherwood Eddy galvanized young people to take the good news of God's light "to those who sit in darkness"—a phrase I remember from my childhood Sunday school days, that always evoked an African hut full of perpetually immobile inhabitants waiting for a missionary team to arrive and deliver them from their perilous sleep.

For there *was* a perilous note as well, evoked by the image of "brands to be plucked from the burning," or to be less coy about it, those whose eternal lot would be damnation and hellfire if they

Initially given as one of a series of lectures at Santa Clara University in the fall of 1992; later published in *Columbus, Confrontation, Christianity,* ed. Timothy O'Keefe (Milwaukee: Forbes Mill Press, 1994), 191–201.

142

did not hear the word of redemption that would lead in the afterlife to an eternity of bliss, with harps for the musical and messianic banquets for the hungry.

So there was good news and bad news. The impetus for evangelization was twofold: a decision for all *eternity* had to be made within the confines of *time,* with no second chances. The stakes were high. One of the leaders used to hold up a pocket watch, counting off the seconds, and citing the equivalent number of those who had been denied salvation because the news had not reached them in time.

However, among many missionaries and missiologists the hard line began to show some cracks. It was difficult, when one thought about it, to believe that salvation depended on geography or chronology—if you lived in a part of the world where the missionary enterprise had not yet penetrated, how could you be blamed for your lack of belief? You belonged to a different category: those who, *if* they had heard the word *would* have responded positively and thus been excused from eternal damnation.[3]

In addition to the geographical/chronological escape clause, as missionaries got to know "natives" in other climes, they discovered many of them to be admirable people, living not dissolute, hateful lives but disciplined and loving lives, without benefit of Christ or clergy. What about them? There appeared to be some "points of contact" between Christians and non-Christians, such as a shared humanity and an innate moral sense of right and wrong. Indeed, forms of what Christians called "the Golden Rule" kept cropping up all over the place in alien cultural settings. Perhaps language was imprecise, and the *same* God was ruler over all people no matter what *name* they attributed to him (it was still a masculine world)— a viewpoint going back to Paul's sermon on Mars Hill, in which he appealed to the Greeks by saying that the God they ignorantly worshiped was the one he was proclaiming to them as the God revealed in Jesus Christ.[4]

An overall image depicted this nineteenth-century outward thrust as a movement "from the center to the periphery." Whether the actual phrase was in common use or not, what was behind it was, of course, a value-laden conviction: The center was where "we" were, and the periphery, the far reaches of the world, was where "they" were, and the traffic went only one way. We had a message to give to them, but they had nothing to contribute to us.

I must acknowledge in all honesty that the rival faiths from which the Protestant missionaries were trying to save their potential constituencies were not only those of the Buddhists and Moslems, but the "papists" as well. Happily, in our day, the ecumenical spirit is well nurtured on the mission field, often more so than back home. As a Protestant observer at the Second Vatican Council, I want to pay special tribute to the "missionary bishops," particularly from Asia and Africa, who had learned that Christians must work together, not only to embody mutual respect, but as the best way to use whatever resources were available in parts of the world where Christians were a tiny minority.[5]

From Outside In

I have spent this time on "the way it was back then" because in many parts of the world that is "the way it still is." If I may employ a Catholic word to describe a Protestant reality, it was "triumphalism" that long dominated the missionary frontier, best epitomized by Stokeley Carmichael's comment about missionaries in Africa: "When they came to Africa we had the land and they had the Bible; now they have the land and we have the Bible." The very image we have employed, "from the center to the periphery," left no doubt who was really in charge.

But there is more to the story, for the inner regenerative power of the gospel burst the bounds people tried to impose on it.[6] As new generations of Christian converts began to grow up in the mission areas, many missionaries were foresighted enough to see that their new task was to relinquish the control and power with which they had arrived, and turn the leadership over to the indigenous Christians. Save among ultra conservatives, the paternalism of white, Western leadership has been replaced by leadership drawn from those who only a generation earlier were "those who sat in darkness."

Furthermore, there has been a recognition that evangelization is not just a verbal message about making it into the *next* world but an enacted concern about living in *this* one. Missionaries did not go just as preachers or dispensers of the sacraments, but as educators, scientists, doctors, and agricultural experts. If they built churches, they also built hospitals and schools. That, too, was evangelization—ministering to the whole person.[7]

There has also been an increasing recognition that many of the symbols, liturgies, and theological reflections of indigenous peoples contribute to, rather than diminish, one's own understanding of Christianity. A Catholic expression of this fact is found in the acknowledgment that the Virgin of Guadalupe is not a wealthy white Hispanic lady of nobility, but a "native" dark-skinned peasant woman without the expected social graces.

What seems to be the decisive movement in evangelization today, to which these brief examples point, is that the overall thrust is reversing. Instead of talking about the gospel going from the center to the periphery, it is more accurate to describe it as a movement "from the periphery to the center."[8] Some have called this "reverse evangelism," that is, those who were once the objects of the evangelistic enterprise are now acquainting us with fresh understandings of the gospel, drawn from their own situation rather than from ours. A good symbol of this is the changing nature of the leadership of the World Council of Churches. At the time of its founding in 1948, the leadership was almost exclusively the Old Boy Network from Europe and North America. But the recent General Secretaries (the top post) have included Philip Potter, a Caribbean black and Emilio Castro, a Latin American Hispanic. Leadership of the various commissions is more and more placed in third-world hands. The pronouncements of the World Council include sharp words of judgment against first-world economic and political policies, especially attempts to suggest that the structures of capitalism are the way to ensure justice.[9]

Evangelism and Good News

The reference to the World Council leads to a turn in a different direction to locate one of the major confusions about evangelization. This is illustrated by a question directed at me during a gathering of conservative Christians: "Are you an ecumenical or an evangelical?" To the questioner, the words were code words for two utterly different views of the gospel.

145

An "ecumenical" was not only an adjective transformed into a noun, but a person mainly concerned about social action done in conjunction with people whose understanding of the gospel was either deficient or nonexistent, so that the truth was distorted, and even hobnobbing with the aforementioned "papists" was not considered out of bounds. According to this reading, ecumenicals were trying to change the world by their own puny efforts rather than leaving all that to the grace of God.

An "evangelical," on the other hand . . . ah, this was a Christian who had made "a personal commitment to Jesus Christ as Lord and Savior" (the exact form of the words is quite important), had dedicated his or her life to "fulltimechristianservice" (one word), and heard the gospel mandate as a commitment to share her or his faith with *any* who were not self-avowed Christians—a new crop of "brands to be plucked from the burning." "Evangelicals," on this reading, were not social-action types but those committed to converting individuals so that their lives were focused on Christ rather than social experimentation.

Let me acknowledge that the above contrasts are something of a caricature, and I do not want to put down the dedication and insight of many evangelical Christians, whose personal faith puts mine to shame. I think of such groups as the "Sojourners" in Washington, and I would be glad to be a follower under their leadership in many of the causes to which they are so fully committed. But I let the contrast stand (at least provisionally) since to many, perhaps particularly to Catholics, a word like "evangelist" conjures up images of Pat Robertson spewing hatred against gays and lesbians at the Republican convention, or Jerry Falwell calling Desmond Tutu, the courageous Anglican archbishop in South Africa, a "phony," or Billy Graham (who is a cut above the rest) still ending finally with a belief that individual conversion is the sum and substance of the good news.[10]

Once upon a time, one could have called these people "apolitical," and indeed *they* were the ones who insisted for generations that "religion and politics don't mix." But they have changed their tune. Now they say to us, "*Your* religion and politics don't mix, but *ours* does"—and hold rallies about prayer in public schools, or building more nuclear weapons to stamp out the godless communists, or moving far beyond nonviolence in attempts to close abortion centers.

How are we to emerge from this theological jungle? I think we need to recapture words like "evangelical" and "evangelism" and "evangelization," from the Christian right wing (whether named Pat Robertson or Opus Dei). After all, the word *evangelion,* from which such words come, is Greek for "gospel," which is Old English for "God's spiel," or what God says and does (since with God no distinction between saying and doing is possible). We redeem them, I believe, when we see that their attention to personal salvation is truncated and misleading unless it is *also* seen as the other side of the coin of social engagement and working for justice. The good news is not just about individual souls; it is about whether or not poor people have soles on their shoes. It is not about fitting into a political or economic system without complaint, but about challenging the structural injustice of those systems. It is not about Brotherhood Week once a year, but about an ongoing challenge to social systems that allow racism to thrive. It is not about uncritical support of George Bush's various wars, but about challenging political systems that make it so easy to engage us in wars on the whim of our leader. It is not about uncritically turning our political decisions over to the politicians on the ground that they know better, but about saying "no!" to political and economic structures that demand, threaten, and finally kill defenseless human beings. It is not about checking in to see which party platform does or does not contain the three letters, G-O-D, but about making tough choices between candidates based less on words and more on deeds. It is not about voting once every four years but working at the local level, on a university campus and/or on the East Side Project to see that injustice finds no place to thrive locally. All that is "evangelization," whatever words are used.

The kind of evangelization that makes sense today is the kind practiced by Bartolomé de las Casas, a Roman Catholic who five hundred years ago went to the New World and sided with the Indians.[11] Las Casas saw that *evangelism cannot be separated from the struggle for justice,* and that it must be engaged in without use of force. That is my theme in one sentence. This does not deny the importance of people's individual lives being

147

changed. But as a total position, the latter is seriously deficient, for it enables its practitioners to focus so exclusively on inner change that they never have to confront the nitty-gritty issues of social justice. By the time they change enough people to begin to think about changing society, a whole generation has gone by, and the whole process must be started all over again.

But if it is not enough to say, "Let us change individuals and then they will change society," it is equally short-sighted to say, "Let us change society and then individuals will be changed." T. S. Eliot has a brutally accurate line about people "dreaming of systems so perfect that no one will need to be good."[12]

The obvious conclusion is that we have to be embarked at every moment on a twofold interlocking task: working to change both the individual *and* the society, or we will either have a terrible world with a handful of exemplary human beings, or terrible human beings unequipped to respond to genuine social need.

So what else is new? Such a conclusion may sound like what the *New Yorker* calls "The Department of Anti-Climax." But it is a crucial point, for the Christian temptation is always to shove the social justice concerns off to the side and say, "We'll get around to that once we get our own inner lives back on track," or even "Don't bother me with politics until I figure out why I hate my father." Contemporary and future patterns of evangelization must *keep individual and social concerns interrelated.* Without that foundation, both our individual and our social concerns will founder.

The New Church

To conclude, I offer a few brief projections for the future. What might be the shape of a Christianity defined by a new form of evangelization?

1. We will be *lay-centered.* The "base communities" in Latin America will be a model to which other parts of the church will be beholden.[13] The Bible, freed up from the rigidity which earlier evangelists imposed upon it, will be used creatively, much as the fisherfolk of the island of Solentiname have placed us in their debt by an ability to relate events in biblical times to

their own times. They have no textual "apparatus"—only a commitment to say to one another what they hear the text telling them.[14] No bishop tells them, "Ours is the only correct interpretation, so reshape your thinking," nor will new church leaders, by whatever name, be able to do so in the future.

2. We will be those who are first of all *listeners*. We are discovering that we don't have as many answers as we once thought. Instead of stonewalling with old answers we must truly open ourselves to hear other voices particularly (for folks like us) from the third world, and not only the third world abroad but the third world within our own community and our own university.

3. We will understand the center of our faith, *Jesus of Nazareth,* in new ways.[15] The triumphal images of Christ seated on a throne wearing a crown will be less prevalent than those of the "man of sorrows and acquainted with grief," making his home among the poor. Nevertheless (or perhaps for that very reason) this will give new meaning not only to old titles—Logos, Savior, Mediator, Messiah—but to the long-neglected title *Liberator,* understood in the threefold sense of being a liberator from the power of sin, from the grip of fate, and the dominance of evil social structures. From such a base, people will be empowered to challenge rather than cringe before the forces of evil, and in battle with them we will discover that we are not alone, but that the power of the liberator is liberating *us* in ways beyond our imagining.

4. We will stress the *centrality of community* (for which the word "church" has been our pointer in the past), but it will be a wider community finally—the community of *the whole human family.* We will find our special niches within it—the Church of Our Lady of Mercy, or Fulton Street Baptist, or All Saints Episcopal, or the Santa Clara Mission. But we will welcome each other across such boundaries. We will not understress the differences that remain, but neither will we let them engulf us. We will find that when it comes to concern for all of God's children there is not "a Catholic view" of racism, a "Methodist view" of fiscal responsibility, or an "Anglican view" of church-state relations, which would keep us divided at such levels. When it comes to being available to those in need, what we can do together far outweighs what keeps us still divided. And I

am persuaded that as we join together in *an ecumenism of service* (the new evangelization), *an ecumenism of belief* will gradually, in ways we do not even imagine, be given to us by God.

I close with powerful words from a recent book by the German theologian Dorothee Soelle, describing what she is learning from her time in Latin America, reverse evangelism at its best:

> From the poor of Latin America I learn their hope, their toughness, their anger, and their patience. I learn a better theology in which God is not Lord-over-us but Strength-in-us. In which the miracles of Jesus are not distinguished from ours; we too drive out demons and heal the sick. I learn trust in the people of God. I overcome skepticism, false conciliatoriness, and short-sighted illusory hopes. I practice betrayal of my own class. I leave their spiritual apartheid and move toward the liberation of all. I gain a part; I belong to them. I am less alone. I begin to hunger and thirst after righteousness. I am evangelized, and I sing along from the new person: *Creadores de la historia, constructores de nueva humanidad* [fashioners of history, builders of a new humanity].[16]

NOTES

1. Kenneth Scott Latourette, *A History of the Expansion of Christianity,* 7 volumes (New York: Harper & Brothers, 1937–1945).

2. The phrase is usually associated with the name of John R. Mott, but it was picked up and used by many others. For details of the period, see Latourette, *History,* volume 7; John R. Mott, *Addresses and Papers* (New York: Association Press, 1946).

3. I cite this doctrinal loophole because it is an interesting Protestant variation on the ancient Catholic doctrine of "baptism of desire." If you had known that baptism was requisite for salvation you would have desired to be baptized, but since you didn't know, you could be saved. "Outside the church there is no salvation," but there are occasional exceptions. Further material on kindred issues is found in William Ernest Hocking, ed., *Re-Thinking Missions* (New York: Harper & Brothers, 1932); Hocking, *Living Religions and a World Faith* (New

York: Macmillan, 1940); and Hendrick Kraemer, *The Christian Message in a Non-Christian World* (Edinburgh: International Missionary Council, 1938).

4. See Acts 17:16–34 for the sermon and its aftermath.

5. I have developed this impression in more detail in *Observer in Rome: A Protestant Report on the Vatican Council* (New York: Doubleday, 1964).

6. Karl Reichelt was in part responsible for creating this new attitude. Compare his *Truth and Tradition in Chinese Buddism* (Shanghai: Commercial Press, 1930) and *Meditation and Pietyä in the Far East* (New York: Harper, 1954).

7. The minutes of most Protestant denomination missionary agencies reflect a gradual but deep appropriation of this position.

8. The phrase is now common among third-world Christians. See Sergio Arce and Oden Marichal, eds., *Evangelization and Politics,* translated from the Spanish by New York Circus Inc., New York, 1982.

9. A new emphasis on "multiculturalism" is now emerging that denies pride of place to "Western" insights. This is symbolized by the recent creation of the Multicultural Institute, at the Franciscan School of Theology in Berkeley, California, and is embodied in the writings of C. S. Song, such as *Jesus and the Reign of God* (Minneapolis: Fortress Press, 1993).

10. A sympathetic yet critical biography of Graham helps explain him to outsiders and also positions him within right-wing Christianity. See William Martin, *A Prophet with Honor: The Billy Graham Story* (New York: William Morrow & Co., 1991).

11. The definitive treatment is Gustavo Gutiérrez's massive *In Search of the Poor of Jesus Christ: The Thought of Bartolomé de Las Casas* (Maryknoll, N.Y.: Orbis Books, 1993). George Sanderlin, ed., *Witness: Writings of Bartolomé de Las Casas* (Maryknoll, N.Y.: Orbis Books, 1992), has short selections from his writings. Helen Rand Parish, ed., *Bartolomé de Las Casas: The Only Way* (Mahwah, N.J.: Paulist Press, 1992), is a fresh translation of his most important text. I have a brief introduction to Las Casas in *Liberation Theology: An Introductory Guide* (Louisville, Ky.: Westminster/John Knox Press, 1993), chap. 2.

12. T. S. Eliot, "Choruses from the Rock," in *The Commonplace Poems and Plays 1909–1950* (New York: Harcourt Brace & World, 1962), 106.

13. Literature on the "base communities" abounds. Compare Leonardo Boff, *Church: Charism and Power* (New York: Crossroad, 1985), esp. chaps. 8–10 and chap. 12, which got him into trouble. A creative Protestant assessment is Guillermo Cook, *The Expectation of the Poor: Latin American Basic Ecclesial Communities in Protestant Perspective* (Maryknoll, N.Y.: Orbis Books, 1985).

14. On Solentiname, see Ernesto Cardenal, ed., *The Gospel in Solentiname,* 4 volumes, (Maryknoll, N.Y.: Orbis Books, 1976–1982).

15. There is a new interest in the person of Jesus in all parts of the world. See John Dominic Crossan, *The Historical Jesus* (San Francisco: Harper-Collins, 1991); Marcus J. Borg, *Jesus: A New Vision* (San Francisco: Harper & Row, 1987); Jaroslav Pelikan, *Jesus through the Centuries* (San Francisco: Harper & Row, 1987); Jürgen Moltmann, *The Way of Jesus Christ* (London: SCM Press, 1990). The image of Jesus as "liberator" is strong in Latin American theology. Compare Gustavo Gutiérrez, *A Theology of Liberation, Christology at the Crossroads* (Maryknoll, N.Y.: Orbis Books, 1988), rev. ed., and Jon Sobrino, *Jesus in Latin America* (Maryknoll, N.Y.: Orbis Books, 1987).

16. Dorothee Soelle, *Stations of the Cross: A Latin American Pilgrimmage* (Minneapolis: Fortress Press, 1993), 94–95.

21 Recipe from a New Ecumenical Cookbook

Our faith possesses both continuity and development, and both are necessary. If there is too much continuity, we get mired in the past; if there is too much development, we lose our moorings for the future. Perhaps we could diagram this tension by examining a recipe for an ecumenical future, found in a cookbook that like all good cookbooks uses ingredients already at hand, or easily available, with which to create something new. My procedure will be first to offer the complete recipe and then to keep referring back to it as we examine it line by line.

An Ecumenical Future: A Recipe

Take one world:

> *a globeful of people, most of whom are victims;*
>
> *a handful of people passionately committed to justice;*
>
> *a God overseeing and supervising without usurping total control;*
>
> *an exemplary human life, in which the globeful of people and the handful of people, and the overseeing God, are united, so that that particular human life is uniquely transparent to the divine;*
>
> *a healthy respect for the past and a healthy skepticism about institutions that have an unhealthy respect for the past;*
>
> *human hearts in which anger and love are two sides of the same coin;*

Originally presented as a lecture at Manila and Iloilo, Philippines, in 1988, on the occasion of the twenty-fifth anniversary of the National Council of Churches.

153

a willingness to risk judgments that might be wrong;
and an ultimate optimism combined with a provisional pessimism.
Mix well, and see what happens.

Take one world . . . Our recipe starts with the world—the whole world, the *oikoumene*—the stage on which our human drama is played out. We do not start with our insights, or our hunches, or our vested interests, or our nation's needs, or even a worked-out theological position. We start with a global perspective. This is an expression of an important contemporary theological principle, enunciated by Gustavo Gutiérrez: "Theology is the *second act.*" The first act, he insists, is commitment, commitment to the struggling poor. And this over all perspective leads to our first ingredient:

. . . *a globeful of people, most of whom are victims.* I am talking here about billions of people, from all areas, cultures, nationalities, and linguistic backgrounds. They are diverse, but they have one thing in common: most of them are victims, oppressed peoples, marginalized to the edges of their society and pushed out of bounds by the relatively few with power. You know the statistics: two-thirds of them go to bed hungry every night; fifteen thousand of them starve to death every day; 6 percent of the rest— the citizens of the United States—consume 40 percent of the world's goods. Those are immoral statistics, describing an immoral reality, and we can be sure the victims will not allow these statistics (which represent their own lives and deaths) to remain indefinitely descriptive of them.

We are soft and indulgent unless we start with these realities. And what many Christians are calling the church's need to give a "preferential option for the poor" is one way of beginning to respond. This means that when a proposal for action, or a political platform, is under discussion, we must ask two questions: (1) Will this help the great majority of the human family to escape from crushing poverty? and more important, (2) Will it help the poor to be empowered so that they can begin to participate in the shaping of their own destiny?

Within this global reality is another reality as well:

. . . *a handful of people, passionately committed to justice.* There are no big numbers here, no impressive statistics, no "power" as the world measures power, but there is immense power when people are willing to see things as they really are.

We call such people the church, that community in which people "turn inward" for the sake of being "turned outward," called *in* to be called *out* into all the *oikoumene*. They are committed to justice, for what is just or unjust can be measured by such things as the remark made by a Chilean underground family in describing the future they want: and the only privileged ones will be the children. This is a good criterion against which to measure progress toward a society in which there is a good future for every child and one not far distant from what Jesus had to say about the nature of the kingdom of God, with "childlikeness" as the badge of entrance.

But this "handful of people, passionately committed to justice," is not just the church. It includes many people who are formally "non-church," and whose commitment to justice frequently puts our own to shame. It is exemplified by socialist Eugene V. Debs's comment, "As long as one person is in prison, I am not free," and by the action of a Sandinista leader, Tómas Borge. Borge, when confronted with the man who had tortured him and killed his wife, was offered the chance for revenge. Instead, he looked at his torturer and said, "My 'revenge' is to forgive you."

We start with such people.

The next part of the mix is

. . . *a God overseeing and supervising without usurping total control.* This is the hardest part—and the most important part—of the ecumenical vision. I believe we must say that God is not in "total" control, at least as we normally understand that term. A God who was in total control would be a cruel God, willing the death of children, sending tornadoes at whim, distributing cancer indiscriminately, helping the rich oppress the poor. No, God does not "run everything." Instead, God has made the risky decision to share power with us, to call us into a kind of partnership, to assign us crucial tasks in the fulfillment of the divine purpose.

This means, among other things, that it is not our job to "take God" to the godless world, but to be the ones who discern those places where God is *already* at work, and was there long before we got there. At one time people might have said, "God comes to the church so that the church can take God to the world." But surely the sequence should be, "God comes to the world so that the church can discern God at work there, and share the good news of what is already happening."

To believe in this God is not to be promised smooth times or easy rewards. There is no guarantee that faith will save us from trouble. In fact, if we truly respond, we are likely to find ourselves in worse "trouble" than before, since our commitments and those of the world will not coincide, but will be in conflict.

So why enlist in God's project? Because the message is not finally about a project but about a person. For part of the mix is

. . . *an exemplary human life.* The starting point in understanding the One who lived "an exemplary human life" is precisely to begin with the *human* life. Whatever else we may affirm about Jesus of Nazareth always comes after that. We know him first as his disciples knew him, initially *in our midst,* as one of us. This means that we can begin to understand how all that we have been affirming so far comes to fulfillment and unity in him. For he was part of

. . . *the globeful of people.* Jesus himself was one of the victims, the marginalized, of whom we have already spoken. In the language of his time, he was one of the *am-ha'aretz,* one of "the poor of the land," living under the domination of a foreign dictator. He was also one of

. . . *the handful of people.* Jesus was part of a minority within a minority. He was a Jew, and to be a Jew in those days (as often it is in our own day) meant to be hated by the others. One reason for this, perhaps, was that the Jews were the minority who were "passionately committed to justice," as the whole prophetic tradition in which Jesus stands makes so clear. The prophets were not appreciated for their critiques of society, and neither was Jesus. And neither are Jews or Christians or any others who are determined to challenge the status quo in any age. But Jesus also showed us

. . . *the overseeing God.* People soon discovered that they could not adequately describe Jesus of Nazareth in exclusively human terms. Without negating his full humanity, they felt compelled to go on and say, in a variety of ways, that in the life of this person, God was also present—as much as it is possible for God to be present in a human life without negating its humanity. The life, death, and resurrection of Jesus represent God's decision to share in the human lot rather than remain aloof from it, and to be present not just as an idealized version of "humanity" in general but as a specific, particularized first-century Jew.

In him, then, all the above

. . . *are united.* In him we see more clearly the nature of the globeful of people, the handful of the justice-oriented people, and the best clues we have concerning the overseeing God. The last point is important enough to need further emphasis:

. . . *that particular human life is uniquely transparent to the divine.* We take such a claim too much for granted. It ought to stun us, and even to shock us at first. How amazing; the human is the vehicle of the divine; the ordinary is the revealer of the extraordinary; the particular shows us as much as we can know of the universal. And the one on whom all these claims center did not come from a big city like Manila or Iloilo, but from a rural village few people had ever heard of and even fewer people had ever visited.

The Fourth Gospel summed it up: "The Word [that is, the creative power of God] was made flesh and pitched his tent in our midst." To the people who first heard those words, the message was a scandal. "Gods" remain in "heaven," sacred beings having nothing to do with secular bodies. Spirits, after all, do not mingle with flesh. And the message to us is clear, even though we don't want to hear it: if God is willing to enter the world as a human being and live and love and suffer within it, we have to do the same thing. We must live and love and suffer within it rather than seek to keep ourselves uncontaminated by all the muck, evil, sin, and terror. We have to pitch our tents here, too. In order to do this wisely, we have to cultivate:

. . . *a healthy respect for the past.* We have a history. The "Jesus Movement" got started a long time ago. It had its ups and downs, and we have to learn how to experience the ups and avoid the downs. The philosopher George Santayana once said, "Those who forget the past are doomed to repeat it." Good news. We don't have to make all those mistakes again. We could even go beyond Santayana and claim that "those who remember the past can sometimes improve upon it." It is what we remember that defines who we will be. In the long history of the Jesus Movement there have been both rogues and saints after whom we can model ourselves: Renaissance popes *or* John XXIII; Grand Inquisitor Torquemada *or* Dorothy Day; Ronald Reagan *or* Martin Luther King Jr.; Johann Sebastian Bach *or* Adolf Hitler; Jesus of Nazareth *or* Herod and Pilate. And we can add to this list saints and rogues out of our own history. However, even with the best intentions, we can abuse this past. So we also need

. . . a healthy skepticism about institutions that have an unhealthy respect for the past. We can get locked into dead forms, outmoded words, stagnating customs. The faith must be "traditioned," which means "handed on," but that mustn't mean slavish imitation in which the spirit is killed so presumably, live. And the forms, so inherited, slay us.

Two things must be kept in living tension here. On the one hand, there is a "Jesus Christ . . . the same yesterday, today, and forever," as the letter to the Hebrews reminds us. But there is also the fact, as Paul reminds us, that "we have this treasure in earthen pots, so that the transcendent power belongs to God and not to us" (2 Cor. 4:7). The forms (the "earthen pots") in which we have the faith are not themselves the faith. They are helps, some good, some not so good, that keep us in contact with a living reality. Old forms sometimes need to be discarded and new forms created in their place. Otherwise tradition, rather than being a good thing, becomes, as someone once defined it, a way to ensure that "the dead always outvote the living."

There is no statement, no formula, no creed, no picture, that does more than hint at the truth it is trying to convey. So we need always to keep writing new creeds, new hymns, new sermons, that tell us in the language and experiences of our time about this Jesus Christ who is the same yesterday, today, and forever. We are most alive when we are drawing on the *past* for new perceptions in the *present* that can shape the *future.* Otherwise we stagnate.

This could cause us to become very cerebral or "intellectual." So we need something more. We need

. . . human hearts in which anger and love are two sides of the same coin. Anger is not the same thing as hatred. Hatred is inclusively destructive; it destroys the hater as well as the object of the hatred, and nobody cares. But

anger (which we are usually told to avoid) may be something we need to recover. By anger I mean things like outrage at injustices to helpless people; unwillingness to accept the way things are for the great majority of the human family; and a commitment to struggle against human rights violators, government graft, U.S. imperialism, and so on.

The second psalm gives us a good, if difficult, handle on this. "Be ye angry," we read, "and sin not" (Psalm 2:4). The first part is easy, particularly if we are given biblical warrant for it, but the second part is very difficult, so difficult that we sometimes forget that it is essential. To be sinfully angry, I suppose, would be to seek to bring about the destruction, rather than the conversion, of the object of our anger, what we might call the Jonah syndrome, which he embodied with considerable success. The Bible, as Gustavo Gutiérrez reminds us, does not tell us to "have no enemies" but to "love our enemies." Yes, we will have enemies, because there will be people who do evil things and we must oppose them. And their welfare must remain an important item on our agendas.

Such anger is the other side of love. It is an act of love to oppose tyranny, an act of love to side with victims of human torture, and thus against the torturers. There are no easy answers here, but to struggle with the problem is one of the most important exercises in which we can engage. And that leads to another ingredient in our recipe:

. . . *a willingness to risk judgments that might be wrong.* We frequently assume that we can be "neutral," and people often argue that the church should not get "involved" in matters of economics or politics. But that doesn't work. Not to decide *is* to decide; it is to give one's vote to whoever has the power in the struggle we decide to sit out. In the Philippines, for instance, if you were not actively against dictator Ferdinand Marcos, you were really supporting Marcos, and making it easier for him to retain control. As Desmond Tutu, the recently retired archbishop of the Anglican Church in South Africa, has said, "If a mouse and an elephant are in a contest and you refuse to take sides, the mouse will not appreciate your 'neutrality.' "

Sometimes we do not want to get involved because we simply do not know enough to make informed judgments. Some things are not so clear—

and yet we have to make commitments. We don't know the best way to alleviate poverty even when we are convinced that it should be alleviated. We may believe that there should be a rural electrification project, but not be sure by which agencies and under whose auspices it should be done. We have to study, do our homework, seek help from people who understand the problems better than we do, reflect on a proposed course of action in the light of the gospel—and so on. And then we have to act even though all the evidence isn't in—for it will never all be in. Karl Barth, who had to make a stand against the Nazis, said, "Better something overbold and therefore in need of forgiveness, than nothing at all." And that sounds pretty difficult. So we also need

. . . *an ultimate optimism combined with a provisional pessimism.* In the end, Christian faith is optimistic. Life is a comedy and not a tragedy. Easter comes after Good Friday. But we cannot say those things too glibly (as I have just done), or say them without balancing them against the dark side of our existence (as I shall now try to do). For along the way there is a lot of tragedy—there are "disappearances" of people we love, tortures, deaths, harm to children. There is no assurance offered to us of short-run victories. There is a stubborn note of realism that looks all such things squarely in the face. But we are counseled not to lose heart. And Paul, who knew all about that dark side, could still go on to write, "For I am sure that neither death, nor life, nor angels, nor principalities, nor powers, nor things present, nor things to come, nor height, nor depth, nor anything else in all creation, shall be able to separate us from the love of God in Christ Jesus our Lord" (Romans 8:38–39).

Our lives are tumultuous, so filled with ups and downs that we have a difficult time balancing them. We can't ever say, from the standpoint of faith, that optimism is unchallenged, or that pessimism alone rules the day. We experience both. But the normative words are faith, hope, and love, rather than unbelief, gloom, and despair. We can be realistic about the dark side of the short run—the provisional pessimism—and not be destroyed by it, because we can be hopeful about the long run, that, as the hymn puts it, "though the wrong seems oft' so strong, God is the Ruler yet."

. . . *Mix well and see what happens.* We can never know ahead of time just what will happen. Disasters become possibilities for victories. Certain kinds of presumed victories go hollow. But we can always live with expectancy.

A story rather than an exhortation will help me make my point. It is a few weeks after the crucifixion. Some of the disciples have sneaked out of Jerusalem, fearful that what happened to their leader will also happen to them, and they have a healthy aversion to crosses as dwelling places. They go back up to the Sea of Galilee and begin to get the family fishing business going again, after its long decline because of their unexpected departure a couple of years earlier to follow a wandering rabbi. And finally the nets are mended, and good relations with the family have been reestablished, and then one day Philip and Bartholomew come over the hill, down to the lakeside, and say, "Hey! He's risen!"

And the first reaction of the disciples has got to have been, "*Oh, no!*" For if he's risen, then it's back to the road again, taking risks, getting jeered at, maybe crucified, or at least imprisoned. It means that the dream wasn't a vain one, and all the talk about the kingdom of God had the stuff of reality and truth about it. But at what a price . . .

So let's grant these disciples the authenticity of their initial cry of despair, that having just gotten their lives together again, they were about to be torn apart. But the "Oh, no!" was gradually transformed into an "Oh, yes!" because if he *is* risen, then to go back on the road is not to go back on the road alone, but with him. To take risks is more entertainable, because he will be with them. And even if death looms, he has shown them that death isn't the end.

The Easter story, in other words, isn't a Hollywood ending tacked onto a tragedy. It is the story of a reality that is not just consoling but also demanding. Demands for new agendas, new dwelling places, maybe sometimes *no* dwelling places, but in which the provisional pessimism is surrounded by an ultimate optimism.

And for that we can only say, "Thanks be to God! Amen."